THE REVOLUTION OF
PETER THE GREAT

G. S. Musikiisky, *Family Portrait of Peter I,* 1720. Pictured with Peter are his wife Catherine, their daughters Anna, Elizabeth, and Natalia (at Catherine's knee), and the future Emperor Peter II, the tsar's grandson.

The Revolution of
Peter the Great

JAMES CRACRAFT

HARVARD UNIVERSITY PRESS
Cambridge, Massachusetts
London, England

Frontispiece: G. S. Musikiisky, *Family Portrait of Peter I,* 1720.
Miniature in oil on enamel on copper base.
(Walters Art Gallery, Baltimore)

First Harvard University Press paperback edition, 2006

Library of Congress Cataloging-in-Publication Data
Cracraft, James.
The Revolution of Peter the Great / James Cracraft.
p. cm.
Includes bibliographical references and index.
ISBN 0-674-01196-1 (cloth)
ISBN 0-674-01984-9 (pbk.)
1. Peter I, Emperor of Russia, 1672–1725.
2. Russia—History—Peter I, 1689–1725. I. Title.

DK131.C73 2003
947'.05—dc21
2003049917

Contents

Preface   *vii*

1   Peter and Company   *1*
2   Military and Naval Revolutions   *29*
3   Diplomatic and Bureaucratic Revolutions   *54*
4   Cultural Revolution   *75*
5   Revolution and Resistance   *114*
6   St. Petersburg   *135*
   Conclusion   *157*

   Chronology   *169*
   Notes   *173*
   Further Reading   *185*
   Index   *189*

Preface

This book condenses for students and general readers my more extended scholarly studies of the reign in Russia of Peter I "the Great." In it, as before, I take the position that what happened of greatest historical significance during this long and ever controversial reign was not the achievement for Russia of the great-power status acclaimed by succeeding generations of historians, politicians, and publicists. Nor was it Peter's modernization of the Russian army, creation of a navy, secularization of the church, foundation of St. Petersburg, or establishment of an absolute monarchy in Russia, momentous as they were. Rather, it was all of these and something more, something that linked together these major historical developments and yet transcended them. That something, I argue, was a cultural revolution, one that I documented at considerable length in three separate volumes, two devoted to visual culture (architecture and imagery), the other to linguistic matters (see Further Reading). But those volumes are much longer and far more detailed than would be needed by beginning students or the interested general reader. Hence this little book.

Peter the Great remains the single most important figure in all of Russian history, a status that makes him, given Russia's importance in the modern world, one of the most important figures in all of modern history. As such, he and his reign have generated an enormous historical literature in Russian, English, and other languages. In condensing my own books here I have tried to incorporate some of the fresh detail and different perspectives to be found in the most recent additions to this literature. But it should be stressed that this book is neither a comprehensive narrative of Peter's reign nor a biography of Peter himself, both of which are readily available. The book is, rather, an interpretive history of the Petrine era, one that is concerned to present in concise and easily readable form the most significant aspects of Peter's reign in Russia—those whose consequences were felt long afterward, indeed, are still with us today.

A note on technical matters: My transliterations of Russian words follow the standard Library of Congress system, here simplified for general readers, except when a proper name is already familiar in a standard English form (hence "Peter," not *Pëtr* or *Pyotr;* "St. Petersburg," not *Sankt-Peterburg*). Dates are given in accordance with the Julian or Old Style calendar used in Russia from Peter's time, which in the eighteenth century was eleven days behind the Gregorian or New Style calendar that was gradually superseding it in Europe (Russia finally adopted the New Style calendar, now used throughout the world, in 1918). The notes to each chapter identify books or articles containing further information on a particular subject or the source of a particular quotation or fact. All other names, dates, facts, and figures found in the book are taken from my own and the other scholarly works listed among the Further Reading suggestions.

For their support in bringing this book to fruition, I am greatly indebted to the Trustees of the University of Illinois, whose grant of a sabbatical leave in spring semester 2002 gave me the time to write the final draft. I am also much indebted to Kathleen

McDermott, senior history editor at Harvard University Press, and to her anonymous readers for their expert advice on revising the manuscript for publication. A deeper debt in preparing the book is to the students in my successive courses on Russia under Peter the Great given at the University of Illinois at Chicago. They both emboldened me to proceed with the project and moderated my pretensions. Finally, I would like to dedicate the book to my wife, Nancy, who was its first reader and whose suggestions for improvement were invaluable.

THE REVOLUTION OF
PETER THE GREAT

I

Peter and Company

Peter became "the Great" in Russia—*Pëtr velikii*—because of the successful revolution he led. In doing so he did not, of course, act alone. No ruler ever does, not even the "Sovereign Tsar and Autocrat of Moscow and All Russia." By longstanding tradition the tsar (or king) ruled in conjunction with a group of senior nobles (the *boiarskaia duma*, or boyars' council), their decisions implemented by a welter of subordinate offices located in Moscow and the chief provincial towns. These offices had emerged over the centuries as outgrowths of the ruler's own household. They performed a variety of often overlapping functions connected with raising taxes, recruiting soldiers, and administering justice. The senior nobles, who met in council with the tsar, controlled at his behest the most important of these offices, commanded his armies, and administered—or "fed off," in the colorful old Russian phrase—the provinces. From time to time, as in the later reign of Peter's father, one or more of the tsar's favorites would dominate his government; at other times the tsar himself personally took charge, enmeshed though he continually was in an elaborate, quasi-religious, Byzantine-like court ceremonial.

There were no institutional or legal limits on the power embodied in the tsar and exercised by himself, the leading boyars, and their many kinsfolk, clients, and subordinate officials and clerks. Except for the "Time of Troubles," the period of dynastic struggle and civil war that raged in Muscovy between 1598 and 1613, the system had succeeded in maintaining political stability and preserving the power and privileges of the ruling elite. Once securely on the throne, however, Peter radically reformed this system in accordance with current European principles of bureaucracy and absolute monarchy. And he did so with the help of his "company," as he sometimes called it *(kompaniia),* adopting in Russian a common European word.

Peter's company was a motley collection of relatives and ex-playmates, sailors and soldiers of fortune of various nationalities, shipwrights and artillerymen, and scions of both noble and not-so-noble Russian clans. To these were added, as time progressed and occasion demanded, learned Ruthenian (Ukrainian or Belorussian) clergymen, German jurists and other imported scholars, Dutch, Italian, and French artists and architects, a British merchant or two, and a mistress of obscure Baltic origins who later became his wife and then successor on the throne. Members of this company, which at any one time numbered a few dozen or more men and women, assisted Peter in the creation of a Russian navy, the modernization of the army, the foundation of a new capital city, the radical reorganization of the state, and the introduction of numerous, often drastic social and cultural reforms. Some also served as his regular drinking companions and played their parts in his often elaborate entertainments. For many years they constituted, in fact, his court, thus displacing the traditional assemblage of Muscovite grandees.

The origins of Peter's company go back to the difficult, often precarious years of his youth spent in and around Moscow, the fabled old city in the heart of the Russian heartland. Peter's father, Tsar Aleksei, died in January 1676, when Peter was only three. He was succeeded by his eldest surviving son, Tsar Fedor III, who took nominal charge of the rest of Aleksei's children by his two wives, the first of whom had died in 1669, the second of whom he had married in 1671. Peter was the son of his father's second wife, Natalia Naryshkina, whose family now rallied around him in hopes that he might one day become tsar and endow them, following Muscovite custom, with the lands, offices, and other perquisites deemed appropriate for members of the tsar's family. But meanwhile, for the same reason, the relatives of Aleksei's first wife supported the succession of his other surviving son by her, Prince (Tsarevich) Ivan, who was six years older than Peter. Peter's chances in this ultimate political game were less dim than they might at first seem. Peter was robustly healthy himself, but his half-brothers were either sickly (Tsar Fedor) or seriously handicapped, both mentally and physically (Prince Ivan). Thus the hopes of many leading Muscovites were vested in Peter should the feeble Fedor die without producing a male heir.

That is exactly what happened in April 1682, when Tsar Fedor died childless. Peter, now almost ten, was proclaimed tsar later the same day by a conclave of nobles, officials, and townsmen hastily convoked in Moscow by Patriarch Joachim, the head of the church. Ivan was passed over on the grounds that his afflictions precluded him from ruling; the patriarch's antipathy to the "Latinizing" (Polish Roman Catholic) influences supposedly rampant in Ivan's entourage probably also played a part. Such an outcome could occur because the royal succession in Muscovite Russia was governed by custom rather than any clear-cut law. It was expected that the new ruler would be an able-bodied male of the ruling family, the Romanovs, whose dynasty had been established in 1613 with the election of Tsar Michael by the "Assembly of the Land" that brought to an end the Time of Troubles. Yet in the only two Romanov successions to date, those of Tsar Aleksei (Michael's son) in 1645 and Tsar Fedor in 1676, the successor had been, in fact, the eldest surviving son of the deceased ruler. At any rate, what soon followed in 1682 may be described as a kind of military coup led, or exploited, by Ivan's older sister (Peter's half-sister), Sophia. The upshot of the whole bloody affair, which claimed the lives of some forty people, including a maternal uncle of Peter's and his widowed mother's protector, both murdered by rioting royal musketeers (*streltsy*) before Peter's own eyes, was a joint monarchy of Ivan and Peter under the de facto regency of Grand Princess (Tsarevna) Sophia. The boys were crowned co-tsars in Moscow in June 1682. A fancy dual throne with a peephole high in its back for Sophia to supervise proceedings, along with a second crown specially made for the occasion, may be seen today in the Kremlin Armory Museum—striking reminders of this altogether unprecedented, and inherently unstable, regime.[1]

The succession crisis of 1682 was symptomatic, as we shall see in a later chapter, of a gathering crisis in the Muscovite polity itself. Noteworthy now is the effect that it had on Peter's career. As the younger of the co-tsars, his mother's "party" excluded from the inner circles of power and his relations with Sophia both distant and tense (his very existence threatened her position), Peter was relegated to the role of junior tsar in the new diarchy and excused from all but ceremonial functions at court. His formal education was also neglected, being left to a series of lesser officials under the overall direction of his indulgent, widowed mother. On the positive side, the relative freedom thus bestowed on the strapping young tsar (he would grow to six feet, seven inches in height, an extremely tall man for his time) allowed him to pursue his hobbies with a passion fortified by his royal status: he could *command* his noble attendants, tutors, relatives, and servants to join him in his military games or to go sailing with him or to carouse until the wee hours. And these were the circumstances in which, during an adolescence spent mostly on the suburban royal estate of Preobrazhenskoe and in the nearby German Settlement, Peter formed his "company."[2]

Among the earliest members of the company were his maternal

uncle, Lev Naryshkin; Fedor Saltykov, whose sister was Tsar Ivan's wife; Fedor Apraksin, the brother of Tsar Fedor's second wife; Tikhon Streshnev, another, more distant relation; Ivan Musin-Pushkin, an exceptionally literate courtier; and Princes Boris A. Golitsyn, Fedor Romodanovsky, and Boris Kurakin, whose wife was the sister of Peter's first wife, whom he married in 1689. Except for Uncle Lev, who died in 1705, all these men came from the senior nobility, some were already seasoned officials, and most were destined to play major roles in Peter's government after he came to power. Other leading nobles who sooner or later joined his company included Peter Tolstoy, who served thirteen years (1701–1714) as Russia's first regular ambassador to Constantinople; Boris Sheremetev, in 1700 named Russia's first field marshal; Fedor Golovin, in 1699 appointed head of the Ambassadorial Office (department of foreign relations) in Moscow and the first knight of Peter's new Order of St. Andrew; and Gavrila Golovkin, who in 1706, on Golovin's death, took over the Ambassadorial Office and in 1709 formally assumed the title of chancellor (*kantsler*, roughly equivalent, on the Austrian model, to foreign minister). Golovkin and Tolstoy were also among the first Russians to receive, from Peter, the hereditary title of count (*graf*, taken straight from the German).

Three foreigners—who lived, as such, in the German Settlement—were also among Peter's favored few: François ("Frants") Lefort, sixteen or so years Peter's senior, a Swiss soldier of fortune who had entered Russian service in 1676; the still more senior Patrick Gordon (born 1635), a Scotsman who had arrived in Moscow in 1661, had trained and then commanded two elite regiments of the Muscovite army and in 1687 was appointed the army's quartermaster-general; and James Bruce (Iakov Brius), near to Peter in age (1670–1733), who was born in Moscow the son of another Scottish soldier in Russian service. In 1683 Bruce joined—or was assigned to—Peter's "play regiment" and seldom thereafter left his side. Both Lefort and Gordon died, as it happened, in

1699, to the young tsar's utter consternation. Lefort had been Peter's boon companion in the German Settlement, introducing him to the delights of European wine, women, and song, had fought with him in the Azov campaigns of 1695 and 1696, and had accompanied him on his Grand Embassy to Europe of 1697–1698. General Gordon had been Peter's trusted military mentor, almost a substitute father, and had played a critical part not only in defeating Sophia's attempted coup of 1689 but in putting down an abortive revolt of the royal musketeers in 1698, while Peter was still in Europe. James Bruce also fought with Peter in the Azov campaigns and accompanied him to Europe, where he stayed behind for a time, in England, to study various technical subjects in preparation for the tsar's service. He went on to distinguish himself not only in military affairs but in various cultural pursuits as well, eventually becoming both count and field marshal and the organizer of Peter's state funeral.

Among the Russians of obscure or lowly social origin who joined Peter's company the best known, or most notorious, is Alexander Menshikov. Very close to his master in age and, like him, tall and physically robust, Menshikov probably first came to Peter's attention as a soldier in one of the elite Moscow regiments that the young tsar would commandeer for service in his war games. By 1693 Menshikov was enrolled in Peter's own, newly formed Preobrazhensky regiment, and by 1695–1696 he was sharing the tsar's tent on the Azov campaigns. In 1697–1698 he too was a member of the Grand Embassy and worked side by side with Peter in the shipyards of Holland and England. He met his future wife at a party given in 1698 by Peter's sister, Natalia, and Peter later met his future wife, Catherine, at a gathering in Menshikov's quarters. In short, by the late 1690s the two had formed a very close, frequently boisterous, sometimes violent relationship that would endure for the rest of their lives. Peter was godfather to Menshikov's several children and in 1705 entrusted him with supervising the education of his own son and heir, Tsarevich Aleksei.

The last line in a note to his "dear friend" of March 1706 is typical of their surviving correspondence: "We are indeed merry here, praise God," Peter wrote, "but our jollity when separated from you is like food without salt."[3]

Menshikov's absolute loyalty to the tsar from the time they were in their teens, along with his energy and versatility, if not ruthlessness, account for his meteoric rise in Peter's service. He achieved the highest military and civil ranks, received several honorary knighthoods from foreign monarchs, and was given by Peter the personal title of "most illustrious prince" (Fig. 1). He also acquired title, by grant of the tsar and of his Polish ally, King Augustus, to some 3,000 villages, various factories and mines, and 7 whole towns located in Russia, Ukraine, Poland, and the Baltic provinces. His palaces in and near the new capital, St. Petersburg, of which he was the first governor, were grander than Peter's own. But Menshikov's rise to great fame and fortune inevitably aroused the envy of rivals as well as the tattle of gossips. Tales of his personal peccadillos and alleged corruption in office periodically reached Peter, who duly rebuked him. In 1718 he was formally charged with embezzling more than a million and a half rubles intended for army supplies, but he got off with a stiff fine. The Russian historian N. I. Pavlenko, a recent biographer, depicts Menshikov as a naturally gifted military commander, splendid organizer, and devoted family man who was at the same time a politician of insatiable greed and unbridled vanity who achieved the heights of "semi-autocratic" power during the brief reign of Empress Catherine (1725–1727), Peter's wife and successor, only to be thrust from office after her death and to die penniless in exile in 1729.[4] Yet an astute English observer of the time, recounting Menshikov's dramatic rise and fall, reminded his readers that despite his shortcomings "the Prince" had long been Peter's able assistant in "all the useful schemes and great designs which the late Tsar had for the improvement and advancement of his country."[5] Menshikov's story has long fascinated Russian writers, painters, and filmmakers, and his restored palace in the center of old St. Petersburg, now a branch of the Hermitage Museum, remains one of the major architectural and historical monuments of the city.

Revolutionary times invariably witness the sudden emergence from obscurity of new leaders, and the Petrine era in Russia certainly was no exception. Apart from Menshikov we can count Pavel Iaguzhinsky, Peter Shafirov, Feofan Prokopovich, and Aleksei Makarov among the upstarts, not to mention Empress Catherine herself. The first was the son of a Polish-Lithuanian organist at the Lutheran church in Moscow's German Settlement whose good looks and knowledge of Polish led to a job in the Ambassadorial Office and then, on Golovin's recommendation, to enrollment in Peter's Preobrazhensky regiment and appointment as one of his orderlies. Distinguishing himself at the critical battle of Poltava (1709), Iaguzhinsky was promoted to the newly created post of adjutant-general and thereafter was rarely out of Peter's sight, eventually rivaling Menshikov as the chief favorite and serving as procurator-general of the reorganized central government.

Shafirov's origins and early rise were somewhat similar to Iaguzhinsky's. The son of a Polish-Ukrainian Jew who had made his way to Moscow, converted to Russian Orthodoxy, worked as a translator for the government, and successfully engaged in trade, young Shafirov became adept at negotiation and foreign languages and followed his father into the Ambassadorial Office. There his skills caught Golovin's eye and then Tsar Peter's. He was a member of the Grand Embassy in 1697–1698, and his ensuing diplomatic career placed him at nearly every crucial juncture of Russia's long war with Sweden for control of the eastern Baltic. After Golovkin succeeded Golovin as chancellor, Shafirov became vice-chancellor *(vitse-kantsler)*, or deputy foreign minister. In 1710, in recognition of his diplomatic efforts in support of the Russian victory over Sweden at Poltava, he was made a baron by Peter *(baron*, also straight from the German), the first Russian to be so honored. Shafirov's subsequent diplomacy on Peter's behalf brought him still more honors and rewards, including the grant of at least two estates, as well as trouble with Menshikov, who in 1722 succeeded in having him convicted of corruption, for which he was exiled. Catherine secured his reprieve, but after her death, and until his own (1739), his career was at the mercy of court favorites. Shafirov's most lasting claim to fame, as we shall see, was as the author of the first Russian book on international law.

The importance of Aleksei Makarov, another of the newcomers mentioned above, derived from his position as the longtime secretary (1704–1725) of Peter's personal office, or *kabinet,* as it came to be called (after the German *Kabinett*). Given the ever-growing range of Peter's interests and the extent of his power, Makarov's job was an increasingly important one as well. Ever mindful of his humble origins as the son of a government clerk, Makarov exercised great but always discreet, and often prudent, influence. He was decently rather than extravagantly compensated for his services by his master, following whose death he retired to the country estate he had been granted. Feofan Prokopovich, by contrast, was a much more public figure notwithstanding his status as a monk of modest social background. Indeed, he was the most outstanding of a group of learned Ruthenian clergy prized by Peter for their loyalty as well as their learning in theology and the Latin and Greek humanities. Such learning was typical of educated clergy in contemporary Europe but was possessed by virtually none of the Russian clergy of the day, many of whom, steeped in Muscovite tradition, were naturally hostile to Peter's rejection of much of that tradition. This gave Prokopovich and his colleagues their opening. Outspoken contempt for what they considered the ignorance and superstition of their Russian counterparts was followed by eager support of Peter's educational initiatives and attempt to reform the Russian church along Anglican or Lutheran lines. Moreover, Prokopovich's many public orations, along with various other writings dating to his twenty years in St. Petersburg (1716–1736), made him the era's most prolific and eloquent champion of the Petrine regime. Some of these writings are thought by scholars to mark the beginnings of modern Russian literature.

Unfortunately, with the exception of his daughter, later empress, Elizabeth, we know comparatively little about the women in Peter's life, the most notable of whom were his mother, Natalia, his sister, also named Natalia, his other surviving daughter, Anna (mother of Peter III), and his two wives. But their importance in shaping "Peter the Great," in enabling and sustaining his achievements and in curbing his excesses, can hardly be doubted. His widowed mother, to whom, their few surviving letters indicate, he was deeply attached, sustained him through the difficult, at times traumatic years of his childhood and adolescence. Until her death in 1694 she stood at the center of the "party" that looked after his political interests in Moscow while he was playing soldier or sailing his toy fleet or carousing in the German Settlement. It was his mother, worried about his chances and alarmed by his unregal behavior, who arranged Peter's first marriage, to Evdokia Lopukhina, a woman who stood by him in the crisis of 1689 and gave birth in 1690 to his only surviving son, Tsarevich Aleksei. Her conventional Muscovite simplicity proved incompatible with her husband's highly adventurous character, however, and his attentions soon turned to Anna Mons, the daughter of an innkeeper in the German Settlement. Anna did much to improve his manners and convert him to Western ways. In 1698 Evdokia was sent to a convent and later divorced, while the affair with Anna gradually waned (she later married a German officer in Russian service). In the meantime Peter's sister Natalia assumed the task of providing a home for his son and heir, a measure of his trust in her. Peter also conferred on her a generous annual income, then a mansion in St. Petersburg and a nearby country estate (she never married, though there were offers, including one from the Austrian archduke). Natalia amassed a sizable wardrobe in the new "German" mode favored by Peter, produced popular European comedies and dramas in her private theaters in Moscow and St. Petersburg, hung a large number of new-style pictures on her walls in addition to traditional icons, and maintained a choir trained to sing in the contemporary Italian fashion. Until her sudden death in 1716 she was Peter's beloved confidante, keeper of his haven from a hard world, and the center of a circle that included Menshikov's sister and wife (and her sister) and Peter's second wife, Catherine. Indeed, while she lived, sister Natalia was the leading feminine representative of the new, Europeanized Russia that Peter struggled to bring into being, her newly sophisticated dress and deportment presenting a stark contrast to the traditional Muscovite habits of her own mother (Figs. 2, 3).

Catherine, successively Peter's mistress, wife, and successor on the throne, is in many ways the most intriguing member of his company. Nothing is known about her early life, but it is likely that she was born somewhere in the Baltic provinces, was probably named Martha, and was raised a Lutheran. At any event, when Russian forces captured the town of Marienburg in the summer of 1702, she was a servant in the household of Pastor Ernst Glück (according to subsequent official publications, the future empress was brought up as his foster-daughter). She was taken from Glück's care to the camp of the Russian commander, Field Marshal Sheremetev, and from there to Menshikov's headquarters, where, sometime around the end of 1703, she caught Peter's eye. Peter called her Katerina or Katerinushka or various other pet names and took her on campaign with him. By December 1706 she had given birth to the first of the at least nine children she would have by him, only two of whom, Anna (born in January 1708) and Elizabeth, the future empress (born in December 1709), survived childhood: the death in 1719 of one of the others, named Peter, aged three and a half, was particularly painful, as he had been proclaimed heir to the throne the year before. It is possible that Peter and Catherine were secretly married in 1707, but their formal wedding took place in St. Petersburg in February 1712.

Peter was dressed in a naval uniform, as was his style, and was attended by Vice-Admiral Cornelius Cruys, a Dutch-Norwegian officer who had entered his service in 1698. By this time, too, Peter's bride had been received into the Russian Orthodox Church and had taken the name Catherine (Fig. 4). Except for her periods of confinement she continued to accompany Peter on his military and diplomatic travels and to share his entertainments, earning from him such appreciation of her fortitude that he founded a knightly order, the Order of St. Catherine, in her honor and later crowned her empress (Fig. 5).

From the time she entered his life Catherine seems to have provided the glue that held Peter's company together. She reconciled him with his closest associates, particularly Menshikov, when they fell from his favor, and she intervened with him on behalf of others, like Shafirov, when they got into trouble. Contemporary witnesses describe how she frequently soothed her excitable husband, restraining his fury. But her fortune as Peter's consort and successor was not free of cost. Not only did she have to endure the frequent pregnancies and the exhausting, often drunken festivities that came with the role, not to mention the ill-concealed scorn of the wellborn; but she also lived in constant fear of losing Peter's affection, without which all was lost. Nor was her fear groundless. In late 1724 Peter discovered an affair she had allegedly been having with, of all people, William Mons, the brother of his erstwhile lover and an official of Catherine's court. All might well have been lost had she not been crowned empress in May of that year. Mons was publicly tried and executed, ostensibly for embezzlement and taking bribes, in November 1724. Little more than two months later Peter himself was dead.

One might well ask, Whatever happened to Tsarevich Aleksei, Peter's only surviving son and apparent heir? The short answer is that he died imprisoned in the Peter-Paul fortress in St. Petersburg in June 1718, at the age of 28, shortly after being convicted of treason and sentenced to death. His story, shrouded in tension and misunderstanding with his father and tsar, is a tragedy of legendary proportions and revelatory, in turn, of the major conflicts of the time in Russia. Raised from infancy by a series of governesses and tutors under the supervision of his unhappy mother and then of his Aunt Natalia, later of Menshikov, Aleksei was required to learn German and "German science" as well as the traditional Russian letters and "law" (catechism). Never as physically robust or mentally alert as Peter himself, whose daunting example he was nonetheless expected to follow, he seems to have been destined to disappoint whatever he tried to do, especially as a soldier, a profession in which, his father repeatedly made clear, it was his duty to excel. From the age of 17 or so, evidently unwilling or unsuited to serve at the front, Aleksei was entrusted with various responsibilities behind the lines—to collect provisions for the army, to inspect fortifications, to supervise the conscription of troops, to help repress mutinies. Late in 1709 he was sent for further study to Dresden, escorted by Baron Huyssen, a Baltic German who had become one of Peter's trusted aides. While he was in Germany his father arranged for him to marry Princess Charlotte-Christina-Sophia of Wolfenbüttel, whose sister was married to the incumbent Holy Roman (Austrian) emperor, Charles VI. It was a distinguished match whatever Aleksei's own inclinations may have been, and yet another sharp break with Muscovite tradition (Peter's brothers, father, and grandfather had married only Russians). The marriage took place at Torgau, in Saxony, in October 1711, after which Aleksei was ordered to resume his studies and his work in support of the ongoing Russian war effort. He returned to Russia from Germany in 1713 and was subjected by his father to a series of examinations on what he had learned while abroad, at least one of which he apparently failed. About this time the poor health he frequently complained of was diagnosed as tuberculosis.

From that point on it was all downhill for Tsarevich Aleksei. His marriage to Charlotte, of whom Peter was very fond, was unhappy, and in 1714 Aleksei went so far as to install his mistress, a

Finnish peasant, in their palace. He had become a heavy drinker and took to grousing with various maternal relatives, dissident clergy, and others of the simmering opposition to his father's regime. In January 1715 an exasperated Peter wrote to Aleksei, asserting that since coming of age he had done little to assist him in his many labors: "On the other hand, you blame and abhor whatever good I have been able to do, at the expense of my health, for the love I have borne my people, and for their advantage; and I have all imaginable reason to believe that you will destroy it all, in case you should survive me."[6]

It was tough talk, but of little avail. Aleksei continued to complain of his illness and to excuse himself from various assignments, all the while consorting with dangerous company. In October 1715 Charlotte gave birth to a son, Peter, a potential heir to the Russian throne (the future Peter II, in fact), and soon died of complications. That seems to have been the last straw. In 1716 Aleksei was given the choice either of mending his ways to his father's satisfaction or of renouncing his claim to the throne and entering a monastery. He chose to flee, all the way to Vienna, seeking refuge with his late wife's brother-in-law, Emperor Charles VI. The Austrians, unsure of what to do, temporarily gave him sanctuary while Peter, outraged at Aleksei's behavior and acutely embarrassed in Europe just as he was trying to round up support for a final blow against Sweden, sent agents to bring him back, promising a pardon. It was Peter Tolstoy who tracked Aleksei down to the fortress of St. Elmo, near Naples, and persuaded him that the Austrians would never help him, that he could never escape his father's reach, and that he had better come home now. He arrived back in Moscow in January 1718 only to learn that in addition to being formally excluded from the succession to the throne (by a manifesto of February 3), he would have to disclose all his "accomplices." And so his trial began.

A special "Chancellery for Secret Inquisitorial Affairs" was

established in Moscow under Tolstoy to investigate the case of
Aleksei, and in June both it and the tsarevich were moved to
St. Petersburg for the trial itself. Aleksei and those he named as his
supporters were subjected to the normal Muscovite criminal pro-
cedure: denunciation was followed by interrogation of the accused under the threat or use of torture, the latter usually a matter
of so many blows with the knout (a heavy whip), which was to
be followed by the accused's confession. On June 14 Aleksei was
formally arraigned before a grand assembly of 128 notables; on
June 24, having heard the evidence, the assembly found him
guilty of treason and rebellion and condemned him to death. Two
days later he died in his cell in the Peter-Paul fortress, the victim,
according to the official account, of a fit of apoplexy. It was said
that Peter and Aleksei had tearfully reconciled on his last day, and
Peter was seen to weep copiously at his son's grandiose state
funeral, which was held on June 30.

Historians have struggled to make sense of the Aleksei affair:
what was the tsarevich actually guilty of, and did it deserve the
death penalty? And why, exactly, did he die? Such questions were
of course asked at the time, and persistently afterward, giving rise
to countless rumors, the immediate publication of the official
account of the case notwithstanding. Nor is it likely that precise
answers to these questions will ever be found. The most recent
investigation of the whole affair indicates that Aleksei was indeed
guilty of consorting with disgruntled opponents of his father's
regime and, worse, of seeking Austrian military support for his
claim to the throne.[7] But the actual cause of his death remains a
mystery, although it seems unlikely that he was secretly murdered;
he probably died the victim of his own dissolute life and poor
health, a condition much exacerbated by the prolonged imprison-
ment and repeated floggings he had undergone in the course of
his investigation and trial. Peter had proved to be the implacable
monarch rather than a merciful father, determined to brook no

threat to his plans nor opposition to his rule, even if it came from his own son. Opponents of his regime, whether at home or abroad, were given clear warning.

Few people were actually punished for crimes allegedly committed in support of Tsarevich Aleksei. But to judge from the available testimony, published and still in the archives, as well as from the importance that Peter obviously attached to the whole affair, the circle of Aleksei's sympathizers was wide, and ranged from senior officials in both the government and the church to countless ordinary folk. By 1718, indeed, opposition to Peter's regime, to his increased taxation, conscription, and other impositions, as well as to his own behavior, especially toward Aleksei, was reaching a level that seemed to him to require drastic new governmental reforms, particularly in the administration of the church. We will discuss those reforms in Chapter 3, and return to the question of resistance to the Petrine revolution in Chapter 5.

Meanwhile, it should be noted that historians have also been puzzled by the elaborate entertainments staged by Peter and his more intimate company, entertainments that themselves gave rise to criticism from many of his subjects and thus fueled further opposition. The ordinary roughhouse in which the tsar and his friends regularly engaged while consuming large quantities of vodka, rhenish wine, and good Baltic beer is not at issue now—conduct described, for instance, in 1702 in a letter from an English merchant in Archangel to his brother back in London. The letter recounts a recent visit of "His Majesty and the Court":

> He's no proud man, I assure you, for he'll eat or be merry with anybody . . . He's a great admirer of such blunt fellows as saylors are. He invited all the nasty tars to dinner with him where he made 'em so drunk that some slop't, some danced, and others fought—he amongst 'em . . . None can complain of his frolicks since he himself is allways the first man.[8]

This was Peter at the age of 30, "bluntly" enjoying himself among the soldiers, seamen, and shipwrights with whom he spent much of his earlier reign building or rebuilding, from the ground up, his armed forces. It is rather Peter's parodic masquerades and his whole mock court that historians struggle to understand, spectacles that also seem to have originated in those youthful years spent in the German Settlement and on the nearby royal estates. At one of the latter, for instance, a fortification built for Peter's war games was named the "capital city of Pressburg" and supposedly ruled by a member of his company, Prince Fedor Romodanovsky, with the titles of "Sovereign" and "Caesar," "Generalissimo" and "Her Kenich" ("M'lord King," in Dutch). So Romodanovsky was addressed by the young tsar himself: "My most illustrious and gracious sovereign . . . Your most illustrious majesty's eternal servant, the bombardier Piter [from the Dutch, Pieter]."[9] The city of Pressburg even had its own prelate. Peter's sometime tutor, Nikita Zotov, was hailed by him as "father the great lord and most holy Ianikita, archbishop of Pressburg and patriarch of all Iauza [a local river] and Kukui [a local stream and popular Russian name for the German Settlement, which was situated between it and the Iauza]."[10] This was an obvious play on the titles of the real patriarch of Moscow and All Russia, whose office was thereby mocked.

In fact, the established church was often the target of the company's sport. As early as 1691 Peter and his friends constituted themselves, for the purposes of jollification, the "Most Drunken Council"—a play, again, on the "Most Holy Council" of senior clergy of the Russian church. Prince Boris Kurakin, an unwilling participant, records in his brief history of Peter's reign some of the activities of this group. It was led, initially, by a maternal relative of the young tsar, an "elderly and stupid drunkard" whose

costume was made in a facetious form, not the least bit like the [real] patriarch's: his miter was of tin, in the style of the miters worn by Catholic bishops, and was engraved with the figure of Bacchus stuck in a cask, which was also sewn on the costumes of his retinue; similarly, in place of pectoral crosses they wore earthenware jugs trimmed with little bells. And in place of the Bible they made a book in which they carried several flasks of vodka. All this was used in ceremonies enacted in honor of Bacchus.

This "book," a large wooden box with cubicles for a dozen or more vodka bottles and a space for storing tobacco pipes, its cover painted with a picture of Peter and his mates taking their ease, survives in a Moscow museum. Kurakin goes on to relate how on Palm Sunday, after the customary religious services, "they also held a procession at their pleasure palace [in the German Settlement]. The mock patriarch was led on a camel around the garden and down to the wine-cellar." Similar parodies of the Palm Sunday rites were "also enacted at Pressburg by the mock patriarch and his bishops . . . I may say, briefly, that they involved drunkenness, lechery, and debauchery of every kind." Kurakin describes still other mock solemnities held by Peter and his company at Christmas and Epiphany alongside the traditional religious observances, the leading roles taken by the most dissolute persons available, who were often "beaten, drenched with water, and otherwise abused" or even accidentally killed.[11]

Nor was Kurakin alone among contemporaries in describing Peter's company at play. F. C. Weber, a German diplomat and memoirist, records a "great Masquerade" that took place in St. Petersburg in January 1715 to celebrate the wedding of the aged "Patriarch" Zotov, now a widower, to "a buxom widow of thirty-four":

The company consisted of about four hundred persons of both sexes. Every four persons had their proper dress and peculiar musical instruments, so that they represented a hundred different sorts of habits and musick, particularly of the Asiatick nations. The four persons appointed to invite the guests were the greatest stammerers that could be found in all Russia. Old decrepit men who were not able to walk or stand had been picked out to serve as bridesmen, stewards, and waiters. There were four running footmen, the most unwieldly fellows, who had been troubled by gout most of their life-time, and were so fat and bulky that they wanted others to lead them. The Mock-Czar [Romodanovsky], who represented King David in his dress, instead of a harp had a lyre covered with a bearskin to play on. He being the chief of the company, was carried on a sled to the four corners of which were tied as many bears, which being prick't with goads by fellows purposely appointed to it made such a frightful roaring as well suited the confused and horrible dinn raised by the disagreeing instruments of the rest of the company. The Czar himself was dressed like a boor [peasant] of Frizeland [northern Netherlands], and skillfully beat a drum in company with three generals. In this manner, bells ringing everywhere, the ill-matched couple were attended by the masks [masqueraders] to the altar of the great church, where they were joined in matrimony by a priest a hundred years old, who had lost his eyesight and memory, to supply which defect a pair of spectacles were put on his nose, two candles held before his eyes, and the words sounded in his ears which he was to pronounce. From church the procession went to the Czar's palace, where the diversions lasted some days.[12]

Nor did it end there. In March 1721 the French ambassador related to his superior in Paris details of a "grande assemblée" that had recently taken place in St. Petersburg. At one table sat Peter with his sailor friends, at another, Menshikov with assorted courtiers and diplomats, and at a third, "the patriarch and a dozen priests dressed as cardinals, whose only distinction was to imbibe much wine and vodka and to smoke tobacco . . . The patriarch to whom I refer is a professional drunkard whom they call the Prince-Pope." Later that month the ambassador attended another such occasion, where "the Prince-Pope and his cardinals" sang horribly and smoked and drank incessantly; guards were posted at the doors so that nobody could leave. "Never in my life," the ambassador exclaimed, "have I undergone such a frightful experience." In September 1723, he further reported, Peter and members of his company buried their Prince-Pope at a spot near St. Petersburg "with ceremonies appropriate to that dignity," and proceeded to elect a successor at a "conclave" held at Preobrazhenskoe, Peter's old headquarters near Moscow.[13]

What was going on? The German diplomat quoted above thought that the many such "diversions" of Peter and his company "suffice to shew, that the Czar among all the heavy cares of government knows how to set apart some days for the relaxation of his mind, and how ingenious he is in the contrivance of those diversions."[14] Prince Kurakin also regarded them as little more than occasional "amusements [zabavy]," however gross or unseemly. The French ambassador, by contrast, attributed the spectacles he had beheld to Peter's desire to "ridicule his clergy" and implied that they were somehow connected with his effort to reform the church. Historians since have tended to divide on the question along similar lines, some suggesting an ulterior political purpose, others, that the Most Drunken Council and all its works, the Sovereign of Pressburg and all his court, and any other such activities indulged in by Peter and company were nothing more than entertainments, and as such require little further comment. This is the view taken by one of Russia's greatest historians, V. O. Kliuchevsky, who reminds us of the traditional Russian taste for buffoonery and insists that "with Peter and his company it was more a matter of playing the fool than of creating conscious parodies. They mocked at everything, sparing neither tradition nor popular sentiment nor their own dignity; they were like children who imitate the words, gestures, and even the facial expressions of adults without ever meaning to criticize or insult them."[15] Even so, just as the faces and games of children often reveal their distance from, or discomfort with, the conventions of the adult world, so the specific content of Peter's "amusements" suggests a certain alienation from, and hostility to, the heavily religious ceremonial of the world in which he had been born and raised. Moreover, just as the games of children, especially older children, are also bonding rites, uniting them against the adult world, so Peter's entertainments may have served a similar purpose for him and his company.[16] Such behavior may be evidence, in other words, that from his youth he possessed the psyche of a rebel as well as a taste for buffoonery.

Peter is the first Russian in history, ruler or subject, about whom we know very much. The fame he achieved already in his own lifetime, the result of his many accomplishments and frequently unconventional behavior, ensured that his letters and papers were carefully preserved by officials of his own as well as subsequent Russian governments. His fame similarly ensured that many of the Europeans whom he met in the course of his work and travels recorded details of their encounters and their impressions of him personally in their letters, diaries, and memoirs. Peter was the first Russian ruler ever to visit western Europe or to speak a western European language (Dutch, the lingua franca of the maritime Baltic world, which he apparently began to learn in Moscow's German Settlement). Numerous European artists, and later their Russian pupils, drew or painted his portrait or sculpted his likeness in wax, marble, metal, and plaster. The abundance of surviving Petrine material is also the product of Peter's own quite extraordinary energy and of his many reforms, for he issued many more laws, charters, and instructions than any Russian ruler before him. The surviving Petrine material even includes the more or less fragmentary records of a dozen nocturnal dreams he experienced between November 1714 and November 1716, evidence that is unique of its kind. In fact, the very existence of these records testifies to what might be called the modernity of Peter's mind. Their mundane, purely secular content, their lack of any religious or mystical or would-be prophetic element, distinguish them sharply from the dreams reported in the literature (mainly saints' lives) of pre-Petrine Russia or, for that matter, of pre-modern Europe as a whole. Peter's action in recording some of his dreams, even his apparent interest in them, was extremely rare anywhere in Europe before the later nineteenth century, when the serious study of dreams became a standard component of modern depth psychology.[17]

The years in question—November 1714 to November 1716—marked a critical time in Peter's reign. Much of it was spent in Europe struggling to bring the war with Sweden to a victorious close, one that would guarantee Russia's possession of the eastern Baltic littoral where the foundations of St. Petersburg had been laid. It was also a time when the crisis with Tsarevich Aleksei was building to a boil. These and other aspects of Peter's conscious life are variously reflected in his dream-records, one of which we might consider here. It dates to a night in January 1715, when Peter, though at home in St. Petersburg, dreamt he was "in Iavorov," a small town near the Polish-Ukrainian city of Lwów/Lviv, where he

came upon a high tower; and from this tower hung down a rope, which [he] took hold of. And [he] went up the tower and wanted to go up the spire [*shpits*], but it was smooth, and his feet could not hold and climb. And so, having made some snowshoes, he went up that spire on those snowshoes. And on the tip of the spire had been put an apple, and on the apple, on one side, was the tsar's emblem of the two-headed eagle; and in the center of the apple was its core. Then with his left hand he fixed a flag in this core.

Peter had dictated his memory of this dream soon after awakening to one of the orderlies who constantly attended him, so the record is written in the third person. And in classic psychoanalytic terms its meaning seems plain: it is a disguised or symbolic reenactment of sexual intercourse, indeed of male sexual conquest. But such an interpretation, however valid, is not very interesting historically since we know from numerous other sources that Peter was sexually active, no doubt aggressively so. We then notice, going beyond its sexual component, the specifically Petrine significance of several of the dream's images: the two-headed eagle, which had long been the emblem of the Russian ruler; the flag, the sort of military appurtenance that accompanied Peter everywhere, always at hand; and the spire or *shpits,* from the Dutch *spits*/German *Spitze,* a word newly adopted in Russian to designate an architectural form that was unknown in traditional Russian building but that Peter had lately brought to Russia, most notably on the church of the Peter-Paul fortress in St. Petersburg. The trouble that the dreamer had in climbing the spire, and his improbable resort to the familiar Russian snowshoes (or skis: *lyzhi*), are equally noteworthy. Moreover, several years before, in the spring of 1711, Peter had spent a month in Iavorov preparing for his upcoming campaign against the Turks, a bold undertaking for which he had not been able to secure any military support from the European powers. He had been joined in Iavorov by his dear Catherine, who accompanied him to various banquets and balls hosted by Polish grandees, thus assuming, though as yet unofficially, the role of tsaritsa (queen). It was at this time, too, in Iavorov, that Peter had arranged for his son Aleksei to marry Princess Charlotte, the sister-in-law of the Austrian emperor, a marriage in which he placed great hope. It had been in one way or another a most memorable time for him. And when these facts are considered in conjunction with the images just mentioned, a meaning emerges that goes well beyond the dream-record's sexual

significance. The dream may well represent, in this larger historical view, Peter's lifelong urge to join, by force if necessary, the
European concert of nations. It may well provide evidence, that is
to say, of the depth and intensity of his determination to lead Russia into Europe.

The very abundance of contemporary evidence relating directly
to Peter, together with the unusual, even unique nature of some of
it, has made it difficult for historians to provide, or agree upon, a
clear-cut appraisal of Russia's first emperor. The problem is
reflected in the visual evidence—in those numerous portraits of
Peter painted from life that depict him alternately as a benign
prince in shining armor, a gallant field commander on horseback,
a wise and farseeing legislator, a devoted husband and father, a
conquering hero, and a splendid, but terrifying, ruler.[18] He was,
no doubt about it, all these and more: a truly protean figure in history, one whose form varies with the perspective—the interests
and values—of those seeking to interpret his career. Our focus
here is on Peter the great Europeanizer, on the ruler who decisively
brought Russia, largely for the good, into Europe and the modern
world. But other serious students of Russian history, it must be
admitted, have found in the evidence a much more mixed, even
sinister figure—at the worst, a tyrant comparable to Ivan the
Terrible and the forerunner of Stalin. The problem is com-
pounded by the common practice of confusing the person and the
ruler, of attempting to apply ordinary human standards of
decency or success to the actions of a leader burdened with challenges and responsibilities of a well-nigh superhuman kind. In
short, it is likely that no final judgment on Peter, in the sense of a
universally accepted assessment of his character and achievements, will ever be reached.[19]

Still, a few basic points would not be contested by serious students of Peter. His combination of high native intelligence, great
height and physical strength, and superabundant energy made
him a natural prodigy, later a genius, among his fellow human

beings. From a very young age he was bound to have an electrifying effect—frightening or inspiring—on the innumerable people he encountered in his ever-crowded life. These virtually genetic attributes of his character, combined with his inherited position, from the age of ten, as tsar, inevitably made him a formidable, even god-like figure in his society, one to be feared and obeyed rather than loved or revered. Nor was the moral guidance he received as a child, as far as we can tell, such as to incline him to walk humbly in the Lord and be charitable to one and all. In fact, there is considerable evidence, more than that provided by the records of his amusements, that Peter early in life conceived an intense dislike for the elaborate ritualism that passed for piety in late Muscovite Russia, and especially for the Eastern Orthodox tradition that saw the tsar as a kind of high priest. This aversion opened the way for his later conversion to a view of sin and salvation that sought to supplement or even replace traditional Russian religiosity by the "practice of piety," the latter as taught by the so-called Pietists of western Europe in opposition to the emphasis on institutions, rites, and dogmas of the Reformed, Lutheran, and Roman Catholic churches of their countries. Pietism was an austere, moralistic, Providential, scrupulously Scriptural, individualistic kind of Christianity, at once mystical, rational, and socially responsible. It had flowered in Peter's time especially in northern Europe, the Europe in which he traveled extensively in 1697–1698 and again in 1716–1717. It was also the Europe from which many of his company had come, men who helped him to found the Russian navy, a modern army and medical service, the St. Petersburg Academy of Sciences, and the collegial system of central government including the Holy Synod. The Synod replaced the patriarchate at the head of the Russian church and proceeded to "reform" the latter in implicit accord with Pietist principles.[20]

Peter's pietism, if that's what it was, led him in maturity to place heavy emphasis on the importance of leading an upright life—a point that may surprise those who focus on his often dissolute entertainments or the frequent violence of his ways. Such a life meant, for the mass of his subjects, essentially one of duty and obedience to higher authority, ultimately the tsar's. For the tsar himself, as an absolute "Christian monarch," a phrase that occurs repeatedly in Peter's later legislation, it meant total submission to the will of God, which was to be discerned in the course of events, along with acceptance of the responsibility actively to guide his subjects on the "straight path of salvation," another favorite phrase. This was the message conveyed in the *Ecclesiastical Regulation* of 1721. It was also conveyed in the catechism composed at Peter's urging by Feofan Prokopovich and first printed in St. Petersburg in 1720; the catechism was so frequently reprinted as to become, very possibly, the most widely distributed book in eighteenth-century Russia. Peter's moralism, whether wisely or mistakenly, even cruelly, applied, is perhaps the key to his mature character. It may also be the key to his many social and educational reforms, reforms for which a purely political motive is often hard to find. Finally, Peter's moralism may help to explain why he seems to have been liked, let alone loved, by so few of his subjects.

The circumstances of Peter's last illness and especially of his funeral highlight the extent to which he had become a supremely majestic yet solitary figure among his people (Fig. 6). A recent medical analysis of contemporary descriptions of his physical condition in later years indicates that he suffered from uremia, a sometimes painful malady (owing to severe urine retention) from which he sought various forms of relief, including taking to his bed for prolonged rests.[21] But then contrary to his doctors' advice he would go off on lengthy sailing expeditions and indulge in extended drinking bouts, his entourage ever fearful of arousing his wrath should they voice any caution. His last crisis is said to have been precipitated by a boating accident he witnessed in St. Petersburg in December 1724, when he waded headlong into the icy water intending to save the crew from drowning and chilled himself to the bone.[22] In any event, a month of progressively worsening health ensued. Peter's agony was punctuated by the indecisive, even harmful ministrations of the doctors, the incense and prayers of the priests, and the plottings of his senior associates (an heir had not been formally named). Eyewitnesses report an enveloping sense of dread as Peter lay dying in his study in the Winter Palace, a dread that extended from the palace to the streets of the city as word of his condition spread, a dread mixed with relief, even joy, when death finally came. Among the grieving throngs perhaps only Catherine and their two surviving daughters, Anna and Elizabeth, Peter's personal secretary, Makarov, and Menshikov, his old friend, sincerely lamented his passing.

Peter's funeral solemnities, like his entire reign, were marked by numerous innovations, all designed to emphasize Russia's new status as a European power.[23] Unlike his predecessors, he was not dressed in religious garb and promptly buried, following the customary religious rites, in a church in the Moscow Kremlin. Peter's body, clothed in fancy new-style court dress with military accessories, lay in state in the Winter Palace in St. Petersburg for more than thirty days. The funeral itself began not with a simple procession of clergy, courtiers, and the tsar's family but with a massive parade of troops in new-style uniforms, of uniformed military officers and high officials and their ladies, of Empress Catherine and her court, of representatives of the nobility, merchants, and clergy—all led by trumpeters and drummers along streets lined by thousands of grenadiers, guardsmen, and sailors of the Baltic fleet. The parade featured the late emperor's favorite horse (since October 1721 the ruler was no longer styled tsar or king but emperor, from the Latin *imperator*), the horse led by two colonels, this too in accord with the French, German, and Swedish royal funerals on which Field Marshal Count James Bruce had modeled the new ceremonies. Peter was buried in the church of the Peter-Paul fortress, which he had built. At the conclusion of the service Archbishop Feofan Prokopovich, his favorite prelate, delivered the eulogy. It is perhaps his most famous oration, "one of the master-

pieces of Russian homiletic literature" and "thoroughly characteristic of Prokopovich's wholehearted support of the entire Petrine
reform program."[24] Prokopovich urged his audience, the assembled
elite of the Russian Empire (no longer the Muscovite *tsarstvo*, or
kingdom), to assuage their grief over Peter's death by pondering
the splendid condition in which he had left them, and to give
their loyalty now to "his constant companion in all his labors
and trials," Empress Catherine. "Perhaps no state occasion of
the Petrine era," says the leading British authority on Peter, "was
more suggestive of cultural change than the one which closed
it."[25] It was indeed cultural change that lay at the heart of the
Petrine revolution.

This book, as stated in the preface, is not a biography of
Peter the Great, tempting though it is to immerse ourselves in the
details of his fascinating life. Biography, helpful as it may be in
studying history, is not history itself. History is never about one
person, however important; it is about people and their multiple
interactions, people organized in groups, communities, nations,
and states. This book offers a history of the revolution in Russia
led by Peter the Great—"great" because he led it. It was a revolution that brought Russia into Europe, thus heavily impacting
the lives of thousands and then millions upon millions of people.
In the chapters that follow we will discuss the various phases of
this revolution—military, naval, bureaucratic, diplomatic, and cultural—and then look at the resistance, whether high-minded or
benighted, that it aroused in Russia. The final chapter is devoted
to St. Petersburg, which remains the embodiment, architectural
and otherwise, of the revolution of Peter the Great.

2

Military and Naval Revolutions

Peter's modernization of the Russian army and his creation of a Russian navy both date to the earliest years of his reign—in fact, to his youthful war games and sailing expeditions of the 1680s and 1690s. Both of these major reforms were also closely linked with developments in Europe as a whole, developments we should briefly consider in order to understand what happened under Peter in Russia.

Historians have labeled the first set of developments in question the military revolution of early modern Europe, which involved innovations in weapons technology and related tactics and strategy, enormous increases in the size of armies and navies, and the ensuing bureaucratization by warring states of their armed forces. The introduction and spread of such innovations gradually rendered obsolete the feudal levies of knights in shining armor and their towering, vulnerable castles, which had been the leading elements of medieval warfare. Indeed, the advent in sixteenth- and seventeenth-century Europe of ever more lethal, highly mobile siege artillery, the appearance correspondingly of ever stronger and more elaborate fortifications, the deployment of increasing numbers of professional pike- and then gun-armed infantry, and the emergence of large standing armies and navies complete with sophisticated infrastructures of recruitment and supply together constituted the initial modernization of military power in Europe. Peter undertook his massive reorganization of Russia's armed forces during this initial phase of military modernization in Europe, which came to an end about the middle of the nineteenth century. Then, another set of military and related developments ushered in a new era in the military history of Europe—actually, of the world. It was the era of industrialized "total war" as represented by the American Civil War and World Wars I and II.[1]

In early modern Europe, advances in weaponry, fortification, and troop deployment, combined with increases in the size of armies and navies, produced a virtual epidemic of warfare rather than a single great war. It was an age of prolonged, expensive, and difficult sieges punctuated by pitched battles between infantry units massed in huge blocks and then lines supported by cavalry charges and artillery duels. Naval engagements at sea were conducted sometimes in conjunction with the battles on land, sometimes not. It has been estimated that between 1480 and 1700 England took part in twenty-nine wars, France in thirty-four, Spain in thirty-six, and the Holy Roman (Austrian) Empire in twenty-five. Between 1610 and 1710 Sweden was at war for two years in every three; Spain, for three years in every four. Elsewhere it has been calculated that at least one million men were under arms in 1710, when European armies reached their early modern numerical peak.[2]

What caused all these wars and preparations for war? The logic of military innovation surely was one factor—the "use them or lose them" syndrome. But so too were religious zeal, dynastic ambition, and commercial rivalry (the rise of capitalism and the competitive quest for resources, then markets), along with such perennials as ethnic, civic, or class pride and plain fear, unbridled greed, and human perversity. The ubiquity and frequency of war made it seem normal or natural to people, while the concentra-

tion of power in the hands of absolute monarchs and military
elites (aristocracies, emerging professional officers corps) made it
all the more likely to happen. Yet specialists have concluded that
"dynastic aggrandizement" was the main motor of war in the early
modern period, meaning the relentless pursuit of territorial expansion by hereditary monarchs seeking economic gain and
strategic security against their equally predatory fellow monarchs.
Dynastic aggrandizement does not explain all of the warfare in
question, to be sure—for example, the Anglo-Dutch commercial
wars of the later seventeenth century. But it does account crucially
for the many wars of Louis XIV of France, those of the Habsburg
monarchies of Spain and the Austrian Empire, and those in the
contemporary Baltic region between the kings of Denmark and
Sweden. And it does largely explain the outbreak and persistence
of the "Great Northern War" of 1700–1721 between Russia under
Peter I and Sweden under Charles XII.

Both monarchs were clearly motivated by dynastic considera-
tions—in the case of the famous "warrior king" Charles XII, by
his lifelong quest to maintain if not expand the Baltic empire he
had inherited from his predecessors of the Vasa dynasty.[3] On
assuming the throne of his Romanov ancestors, Peter, in turn,
inherited their claim to certain Baltic territories that had been
occupied for a century or more by Sweden. War between the two
dynasts was as good as inevitable. War against Charles XII, who
was one of the outstanding military commanders of the age,
became the salient feature of Peter's reign. In fact, recovery of
lands that were Peter's by right of inheritance is the dominant
theme of the first treatise on international law ever written in Russian, a book entitled, in its contemporary English translation,
*A Discourse Concerning the Just Reasons Which his Czarish Majesty,
Peter I . . . had for beginning the War against the King of Sweden,
Charles XII, Anno 1700.* The treatise was composed by Peter Shafirov
in 1716 and first published in St. Petersburg the following year. It
demonstrates that in prosecuting the Northern War, Tsar Peter

and his government had fully assimilated contemporary European political terminology and associated legal, political, and diplomatic concepts. The book marked Russian acceptance, in other words, of the norms of international law as then understood in Europe. It also put the blame for both starting and continuing the war squarely on the shoulders of the Swedish king.

Peter also inherited from his royal Muscovite predecessors fluid boundaries and tense relations with both the Ottoman Turkish Empire and the kingdom of Poland. But his struggles with these two powers for new territory or strategic security inevitably became entangled with his long war against the king of Sweden, his rival in what became a war not just for certain Baltic lands but for dominance in northeastern Europe. The prospect and then the reality of war against the Ottoman Empire followed by war against the Swedish king and his Polish allies quickly persuaded Peter that he had to reform his armed forces in accordance with contemporary European standards if he was going to hold his own against these foes, let alone prevail. Indeed, in the years immediately following the disastrous Russian defeat by Swedish forces at Narva in 1700 it seemed that his very throne might be taken from him and Russia itself partitioned among Sweden's friends. It was necessary, Peter early realized, fully to implant in Russia the military revolution that had already transformed the armed forces of the leading states of Europe.

Creating a navy was one major step in the process, modernizing the army was another—meaning the various land forces, standing or on call in Russia, when Peter became tsar. Apart from the semi-regular musketeers *(streltsy)* stationed in Moscow and a few other towns, these forces consisted mainly of traditional Muscovite cavalry units and a few new-style infantry regiments supported by cumbersome or weak administrative and armaments infrastructures. Mustered as they customarily were for a single campaign and then largely dispersed, and heavily dependent on foreign, usually German, mercenaries and military supplies (lead, gunpowder, weapons), Muscovy's armed forces as they stood in the late seventeenth century bore comparison with those of leading European states dating to a century and more before. In fact, the poor showing of the huge Muscovite armies assembled by Grand Princess Sophia and her chief minister for the campaigns of 1687 and 1689 against the Ottomans and their Crimean vassals had been a major factor in Peter's decision to seize full power.[4]

The creation of permanent, centrally managed offices for administering and supporting Russia's armed forces was one important way Peter and his assistants sought to bring them up to contemporary European standards. This reform entailed the establishment of more efficient systems of central command and control, and of taxation, recruitment, training, and supply, together with more effective organization and deployment of the armed forces themselves. Peter thus abandoned the traditional levy of noble cavalry and gradually disbanded the semi-regular, riot-prone royal musketeers, who had constituted virtually the only standing force at the disposal of his predecessors. He then recruited and drilled, at first ad hoc and later in a more fully rationalized way, dozens of new infantry and cavalry regiments, established separate mobile artillery and engineering units, and created a general staff. Elaborate new-style fortifications were built around Moscow and Kiev and at Azov, Archangel, and elsewhere in his realm, especially the St. Petersburg area. In taking these steps Peter drew freely on the expertise of his foreign officers, to be sure, but also on the lessons he had learned in his boyhood war games (Fig. 7), which had merged into his campaigns of 1695 and 1696 against Azov, a Turkish-held city at the mouth of the river Don. The first campaign had been a dismal failure, the second a resounding success (Fig. 8). Nor did his efforts end there.

To institutionalize his military revolution in Russia Peter founded artillery and engineering schools, first in Moscow and then in St. Petersburg. In this way he ensured that the foreign officers (mostly Germans) who initially implemented the reforms would be gradually replaced by properly trained Russians. He also founded elementary garrison schools for the children of his soldiers—some fifty existed by the time of his death—to prepare a steady flow of qualified candidates for the more advanced artillery and engineering schools. Military textbooks were translated from French, German, and Dutch for the use of Russian cadets, giving them direct access to the terminology and concepts of contemporary European military culture. A lengthy *Military Statute,* codifying all the relevant reforms in appropriate new language (mostly borrowed from German), was promulgated in 1716. The *Statute,* based largely on a recent Swedish code, also made extensive provision for the harsh penalties that were typical of the new military discipline being imposed at the time throughout Europe. Annual recruiting levies were introduced to keep the army up to its prescribed strength, and new taxes to pay for it were instituted, the latter culminating in Russia's first universal capitation or "soul" tax, which was collected annually from 1724. At the same time, supporting industries were built up especially in metals, armaments, and textiles, an undertaking that resulted in Russian economic self-sufficiency for military purposes.[5] And the related administrative apparatus was drastically streamlined.

The eighteen Moscow offices concerned with military affairs at Peter's accession were compressed into a single College of War in St. Petersburg, an office that he founded, again with European models in mind, in 1718. The College—so-called because it was run by a board of officials rather than by a single minister—was charged with administering what had become by 1725 a standing army trained, uniformed, and equipped up to the better or best contemporary European standards. It totaled as many as 130,000 men, not including an additional 75,000 to 80,000 garrison troops and perhaps 20,000 Cossack irregulars. It was an army equivalent in overall size as well as technically superior to that of Russia's largest traditional rival, the Ottoman Empire, whose forces had nevertheless overwhelmed it in 1711 at the battle by the

Pruth, a river in Moldavia. That defeat had required Peter to negotiate away the fruits of his earlier Azov victory while redoubling his reform efforts (the defeat was later counterbalanced by Peter's successful campaign of 1722–1723 against the Ottomans' Persian vassals). In sum, Peter's new army had proved capable of advanced fortification and siege operations and of joint operations with Russia's new naval forces. And it had defeated in battle, not once but repeatedly, the forces of one of the pioneers of military modernization in Europe, the kingdom of Sweden. Those victories confirmed Russian possession of the newly conquered eastern Baltic lands, which included the site of Peter's new capital, St. Petersburg.

Still more, Peter's military modernization had important social consequences. In support of his reform he introduced regulations, codified in his "Table of Ranks" of 1722, whereby promotion was to be based on merit and length of service instead of social standing or family connections, which had been the Muscovite custom. According to the Table, hereditary noble status was automatically conferred on any man who reached the rank of major or its equivalents in the navy and the civil and court services (royal court, not judicial court). Other Petrine regulations required most members of the hereditary nobility to enter state service in their youth and to serve at the monarch's pleasure, with promotions and other emoluments dependent, again, on merit and length of service. Such rules were closely in keeping with efforts to promote military professionalization everywhere in Europe at this time, and their effect in Russia was to provide unprecedented access to the officer ranks and even to noble status for men of the lower social orders.

By 1725, when Peter died, something like 12 percent of Russian infantry officers had been born peasants. Still, sons of the nobility continued to dominate the officer ranks of the Russian army, even if they now had to earn their position, and the nobility as a whole had been in effect drafted into state service. This situation promptly became a source of grievance against Peter's regime, and for years after his death the nobility struggled to emancipate themselves from mandatory state service. They finally achieved their goal by a decree of 1762. Peter's link between noble status and state service was thereby severed, leaving the nobility, never more than a tiny proportion of the total population, free to enjoy their unique land- and serf-owning privileges undisturbed by service obligations. Their peasant-serfs, meanwhile, liable to the annual soul tax and subject to military conscription, continued to owe their noble masters various dues in labor, money, or kind, a burden that Peter had done nothing to curtail. Indeed, the emancipation of the nobility in 1762 without a corresponding emancipation of their serfs would only intensify social unrest in Russia, unrest that periodically erupted in violent peasant uprisings. Peter may be criticized for not eliminating or even alleviating serfdom in Russia, the underlying cause of this unrest. Yet serfdom had been instituted long before he came to power, and it would remain in place until the emancipation of 1861, when the Imperial government at last felt sufficiently strong to face down the opposition of the nobility and abolish this hoary vestige of the Muscovite past.

Some critics have also judged excessive the financial costs of Peter's program of military modernization. In fact, one prominent historian considers them far in excess of what the country could afford, with dire consequences for its future development.[6] But this judgment, too, seems simplistic. It overlooks the positive results of the program in terms of diplomatic and territorial gains, which brought Russia into Europe economically as well as politically, particularly via its new Baltic ports of St. Petersburg and Reval. The judgment also appears to neglect the negative results, economic, social, and political, of the very similar military modernizations undertaken virtually everywhere in early modern Europe. Finally, it seems to underestimate the degree to which

Peter and his government had any choice in the matter, caught up as they were in a vicious international power game.

The new Russian army raised, trained, equipped, and led by Peter and his senior officers and government officials certainly played the key role in Russia's defeat of Sweden and permanent acquisition of the eastern Baltic littoral. This achievement was certified for all to see in the formal peace treaty concluded between Russian and Swedish representatives at Nystad, in Swedish Finland, in 1721 (the Peace of Nystad, or Nystadt). But Peter's new navy was also an important factor in Russia's rise to dominance in northern Europe. Moreover the navy, even more directly than the army, was Peter's personal creation; and it symbolized, more dramatically than the army ever could, Russia's new identity. Its story, too, begins in Europe.

By the time Peter came to power in Russia a vibrant maritime culture had flourished for centuries in the Mediterranean, Atlantic, North Sea, and Baltic ports of Europe, where as many as 400,000 mariners, fishermen, and ordinary sailors lived and plied their skills. Technical exchange among these communities in navigational matters, shipbuilding, and related aspects of commerce and administration had gradually promoted a convergence of nautical terminology, mercantile practice, and maritime law as well as the establishment by concerned governments of fleets, shipyards, admiralties, and arsenals. A common hydrography and cartography, along with common standards of naval architecture and the mathematics necessary for all these exercises, had also proliferated in maritime Europe. So, too, however unevenly, had the vessels and instruments of oceanic navigation, the fruits of maritime commerce, and the trophies of overseas empire. Bearers of the maritime culture of early modern Europe possessed their own lingua franca—in the North Sea–Baltic region it was Dutch—and their own distinctive ethos, one of both "solidarity and independence," in the words of a leading scholar: an ethos that was at once religious and reckless.[7] But while Tsar Peter of Russia imbibed this culture at an early age, including a working knowledge of Dutch, it was still wholly alien to almost all his countrymen.

A brief look at the history of the English navy may help focus our view, since it was to England, arguably the leading maritime power of his day, that Peter would turn for help in creating his own fleet. English navigation, it is generally agreed, began to supersede its Continental rivals in the reign of Queen Elizabeth (1558–1603). By the time of her death, and owing considerably to her efforts, a whole department of state had been created to run the royal navy. The navy's officers were highly trained in the complex techniques of navigating a great sailing ship on the open seas, and shipbuilding had become a major English industry. The decade of the interregnum (1649–1660), when the monarchy was replaced by the Commonwealth, saw the next major phase in the royal navy's history: it was then that some 216 vessels were added to its force of about 50 warships, an unprecedented expansion. This huge buildup, motivated by the Commonwealth's need to defend itself against diehard royalists both at home and abroad and by its trade wars with the Dutch, was achieved only in part by the timeworn policy of hiring merchant ships for state service. Far more important was the massive shipbuilding program that the Commonwealth undertook. Warships were produced that were not only well-armed by contemporary standards but also more maneuverable, versatile, and cost-effective than their predecessors. The outcome was a navy that none of England's rivals could match—not France, whose navy had dwindled to 20 vessels by 1661, nor Spain, nor even the Dutch Republic.[8]

Following the restoration of the monarchy the new king of England, Charles II (1660–1685), and his brother and successor, James II (1685–1688), eagerly embraced the policy of English naval supremacy over any enemy or likely combination of enemies. So did William III, the Dutch prince of Orange who was elected to the English throne in 1689 and with whom Peter dealt extensively during his Grand Embassy of 1697–1698. The royal navy in the reign of William's successor, Queen Anne (1702–1714), with whom Peter also treated, was composed at different times of between 185 and 213 warships manned by a total of 40,000 to 50,000 sailors and marines. At this juncture only the navy of the kingdom of France, waxing and waning with the fortunes of Louis XIV, comprised a comparable number of ships. But then the War of the Spanish Succession (1701–1713), arraying England and the Dutch Republic against France, exhausted King Louis's naval resources, as it did those of the Dutch Republic; and England's naval superiority among the European powers, established by 1692, remained intact. This was particularly so in the Baltic, where the royal navy was stronger than all other navies combined.[9]

To be sure, the buildup of England's navy was owed as much or more to the push of moneyed and allied political interests in London as it was to the ambitions of England's monarchs. By 1601 half a dozen overseas trading corporations had been formed in London. The first of these was the Muscovy Company, whose 201 member merchants received a royal charter in 1555 and went on to open, and initially to dominate, the trade between western Europe and Russia via the northern White Sea route, a trade that came to be based at Archangel (founded for that purpose in 1584). Together with the royal navy these trading companies gave an enormous boost to the construction of ever more efficient ocean-going vessels until, as Tsar Peter would discover personally in 1697–1698, English ship design and shipbuilding methods were considered the best in Europe. The indigenous supply of naval stores could not keep pace with all this growth, however, and by the late sixteenth century wood for masts and spars, hemp for cordage, and pitch and tar for waterproofing and preservation had to be imported from the eastern Baltic lands, particularly Russia. These commodities were the stock-in-trade of the Muscovy Company, whose restrictive practices along with vigorous Dutch competition eventually led a concerned English government, ever in need of more naval stores and prompted by Tsar Peter's visit, to pass an Act of Parliament designed "to enlarge the Trade to Russia" (March 25, 1699). Well into the eighteenth century, Dutch merchants and Dutch ships continued to dominate the Baltic trade, as they had since about 1600. But an expansive new era in the history of Anglo-Russian commerce, one culminating by the middle of the century in a British commercial hegemony in Russia, had begun.[10]

English mariners were not among the inventors of the new nautical science that developed in this first great age of European overseas expansion (1400–1715), however, an age characterized more by commercial penetration supported by naval force, both state and private, than by extensive settlement and overt political control.[11] As late as the 1570s there was nothing in England comparable to the School for Navigators established by Prince Henry in Portugal early in the fifteenth century or the similar institution set up in Spain, at Seville, a century or so later. Indeed, the Spanish-born Sebastian Cabot (1477?–1558), a graduate of the Seville school who in 1548 was induced to transfer his allegiance to the English crown, did as much as anyone to implant the new science in England. There he busied himself until his death instructing navigators, drawing up charts, and making navigational instruments. One of his pupils was Richard Chancellor, who in 1553, in a perilous voyage at sea, discovered the northern route to Russia—which in turn led to the establishment of the Muscovy Company and regular Anglo-Russian trade. The next big boost to the development of scientific navigation in England came with the reign of Charles II, himself an avid mariner, who established the Royal (scientific) Society of London in 1662, the Royal (astronomical) Observatory at Greenwich in 1675, both of which Peter would visit in 1698, and, most important for our story, the Royal Mathematical School at Christ's Hospital, also London, in 1673, this last mainly for the purpose of meeting the ever-growing need for mathematically trained navigators. In 1698 two students of this school were appointed by Peter to teach in the school of mathematics and navigation that he would shortly found, on English advice, in Moscow.

It is an ever-remarkable fact, surely, that Tsar Peter himself was the first Russian in history to master the new nautical science and one of the first, if not the very first, to learn how to build a full-scale sailing ship. These seem, moreover, to have been his proudest personal achievements. An important testimonial in both respects is his own account of the "beginnings of this marine business" in Russia, which is contained in his draft preface to the *Naval Statute* he promulgated in 1720. Here we read how his late father, Tsar Aleksei, had taken great care to protect and enlarge his royal patrimony "especially in military matters," and this "not only on land, but on the sea (which was such a strange thing among us, that we'd hardly heard about it)."[12] Peter then cites the ill-fated attempt under his father to build with Dutch help a flotilla of warships for service on the Volga-Caspian trade route, a project that was abandoned when the first vessels were destroyed or dispersed by brigands at Astrakhan at the end of their maiden voyage. Professing resignation to the "will of the High Ruler" in this misfortune, Peter saw in those ships, "in a strange way," the "beginnings, as from seeds, of the present marine business." He goes on to explain how two Dutch seamen, Franz Timmerman and Carsten Brandt, had remained in Russia after the project was abandoned, making their living at carpentry and odd jobs, and had been introduced to the young tsar in the following way. A Russian ambassador returning from France in 1687 had brought Peter an astrolabe, and Timmerman was summoned to show him how to use it. A few months later, when Peter happened to find an old English sailboat in a warehouse on one of the suburban royal estates, he asked Timmerman, now "incessantly in our company," what "advantage" it had over "our boats." According to Peter,

> he told me that it goes by sails not only with the wind, but against the wind; which speech threw me into great surprise and even disbelief. Then I again asked him: is there somebody

who could repair it and show how this is done? He said that
there was. Then I with great joy hearing this, ordered [him]
to find him. And the aforesaid Frants [Timmerman] sought
out the Hollander Karshten Brant . . . [He] repaired this boat
[*bot*] and made a mast [*masht*] and sails, and on the Iauza
[river] tacked about [*laviroval*] before me, which especially
surprised me and was very pleasing. Then, when I often exercised thus with him, and the boat did not always come about
well, but inclined more towards the bank, I asked: why this?
He said, the water [river] is narrow. Then I moved it [the
boat] to Prosianoi pond, but found little advantage there,
while hourly my zeal grew. Therefore I began to inquire,
where is there more water; they told me lake Pereslavskoe is
much bigger, whereto I [went] as if to the Trinity monastery,
as promised to mother; but once there I entreated her to let a
yard and boats be made. And so the aforesaid Brant made
two small frigates [*fregata*] and three yachts [*iakhty*], and
there I satisfied my zeal for several years.

So Peter's introduction to sailing and shipbuilding under the tute-
lage of two Dutch masters, his account of which is replete with
the Dutch or English nautical terms he had learned (italicized
above), sowed the "seeds," as he says, of the mighty navy he would
found.

We know from contemporary sources, including his surviving
notebooks and letters to his mother, that between 1688 and 1692
Peter proceeded from this seemingly chance initiation into nautical matters to the construction, outfitting, and exercising on lake
Pereiaslavskoe (now Pleshcheevo) of a veritable "toy fleet." The
fleet consisted of two small frigates and three yachts Brandt had
built with Peter's help, some sort of warship Peter had built on his
own, and various smaller craft built on his orders at Preobrazhenskoe and Moscow and hauled overland to his new shipyard by the
old town of Pereiaslavl, about 135 kilometers northeast of Moscow.

Brandt died in June 1692, but Peter, ever "zealous" in the "marine business," returned to Pereiaslavl in July to help Timmerman fit out the completed fleet, which in August set sail across the lake under the command of "Admiral" Fedor Romodanovsky and General Patrick Gordon, with Peter himself aboard the play warship of another favorite, "Frants" Lefort. In due course he found lake Pereiaslavskoe too small for his waxing nautical ambitions and so, as he wrote further in his preface to the *Naval Statute,*

> was formed my intention to see the sea directly, about which I began to entreat my mother, that she would permit me; who though in her usual maternal love often forbade this dangerous path, but then, seeing my great desire and unchanging zeal, reluctantly permitted. And so in the year [1693] I was at the City [Archangel] and from the City we went out to sea as far as Ponoi with the English and Dutch merchant ships and a Dutch convoy, which was commanded by captain Golgolsen; and we were on my yacht, named the *St. Peter.*

The "we" in this expedition included a Dutch physician, a Russian chaplain with eight cantors, forty royal musketeers, numerous officials, and two favorite dwarfs. All had departed with their young tsar from Moscow on July 4, 1693, then had traveled overland and by river all to Archangel, on the White Sea, where they arrived on July 30. The annual summer visitation of the Dutch and English merchant fleets was about to end, and, as they sailed off, Peter tagged along in his newly built yacht as far as the mouth of the river Ponoi, a distance of about 320 kilometers, where he beheld the "Northern Sea [Arctic Ocean]." He arrived back in Archangel on August 10 and on August 14, as again later that month and twice in September, he wrote to his anxious mother, who was pressing him to return to Moscow. He assured her that all was well and that he would come as soon as possible.[13] We catch a glimpse in this correspondence of how "strange" indeed was the young tsar's growing nautical enthusiasm in his own domestic setting, let alone elsewhere in Muscovite society.

Undeterred by his mother's continuing entreaties to stay home, in Moscow, Peter quickly made plans to return to Archangel and to sail from there into the Arctic Ocean itself. For this purpose the *St. Peter* and two new ships were to form a squadron: the first was to be built by Dutch shipwrights at Archangel, the second to be purchased in Amsterdam. The trusty General Gordon was appointed "rear-admiral" of the squadron, and in May 1694 Peter arrived in Archangel with an even larger suite (some 300 men) to oversee completion of the *St. Paul,* as the locally built vessel was christened, and to await the arrival in July of the 44-gun frigate *Holy Prophecy,* which was purchased in Holland. Soon the squadron set sail for a three-week cruise in the Arctic Ocean, with Peter himself serving on board the *Holy Prophecy* as a subordinate "skipper [*schiper*]." In notes of the time he began signing himself "Piter," the Dutch form (Pieter) of his name, sometimes preceded by *Bombardir* or *Kapitein* if not *Schiper,* always in Latin rather than Russian letters—further evidence of his personal assimilation of the maritime culture of Europe as well as growing obsession with all things nautical.

At this point in Peter's draft preface to the *Naval Statute* the writing shifts to another hand, apparently that of the frequent collaborator of his later years, Feofan Prokopovich, although interjections in Peter's hand, as indicated below in italics, recur:

> They were gladdened by such fine sailing [at Archangel], though our Lord [Peter] was not content. *Therefore his whole thought was turned to building a navy* [*flot,* from Dutch *vloot/* German *Flotte*], *and . . .* [he] soon set to work. A convenient place for shipbuilding was found on the Voronezh river, below the town of that name, skilled craftsmen were summoned from England and Holland, and in 1696 a new thing

was begun in Russia: the building at great expense of ships, galleys, and other craft. And in order for this to be permanently established in Russia, he resolved to introduce this art to his people, and therefore sent a large number of well-born persons to Holland and other dominions to study [naval] architecture and navigation. And what is more wondrous, as if the Monarch [Peter] were ashamed to lag behind his subjects in this art, he himself undertook a journey to Holland, and in Amsterdam, *at the East India wharf,* having given himself over with other of his volunteers to the study of ship architecture, in a short time he was accomplished in it *as far as it suits a good carpenter to know,* and by his own labors and craftsmanship he built and launched a new ship.

Thus Peter's own account of two critical stages in the actual creation of the Russian navy: the building of a war fleet at Voronezh, with the help of imported Dutch and English craftsmen, for descent down the Don river to support his second and successful siege of Azov, in 1696; and his subsequent dispatch of a group of his nobles to Holland and elsewhere in Europe to learn shipbuilding and navigation, a project in which he personally participated.

Peter's training in navigation and shipbuilding, begun during his youth in Russia, was completed in Amsterdam and London during his Grand Embassy of 1697–1698. The ostensible purpose of the embassy was to secure allies against the Ottoman Empire for another campaign in the Black Sea region, a purpose that was not to be achieved, as most of the European powers were already immersed in one of the era's many dynastic wars. But the approximately eighteen months that Peter and various of his suite of about 250 nobles, attendants, and support staff spent traveling, working, living, and relaxing in north Germany, Holland, England, Austria, Poland, and possibly Venice proved to be a crucial experience both for them personally and for Russia's future. Especially was this so with respect to nautical matters. Peter and dozens of his closest associates spent a total of ten of these months in and around those two centers of shipbuilding and trade, Amsterdam and London. There they hired hundreds of shipwrights, naval officers, and seamen for service in Russia and purchased tons of naval stores for shipment back home. In England, as mentioned, Peter hired the first teachers for the school of navigation that he soon founded, on the English model, in Moscow (later moved to St. Petersburg and named the Naval Academy). Captain John Perry, a naval engineer hired by Peter in England in 1698 who went on to work in Russia until 1712, reports in his memoirs that Peter "often declared to his Lords, when he has been a little merry, that he thinks it a much happier Life to be an Admiral in England, than Czar in Russia."[14] His report is confirmed by one of Peter's longtime Russian associates, Andrei Nartov, who recounts in his memoirs that he also heard his master say, "If I were not tsar, I would want to be a Great-British admiral."[15]

Initially all the shipwrights hired in England in 1697–1698 served at Voronezh on the Don building Peter's Black Sea fleet (Fig. 9). Following the Russian defeat at the battle by the Pruth in 1711, however, most of that fleet had to be surrendered or scuttled and the supporting yards closed. At that point Peter turned his full attention to the St. Petersburg region and the buildup of his Baltic fleet. Some fifty-four ships of the line were built there mainly under British shipwrights between 1708 and 1725; so was a sizeable oar-powered galley fleet, for the building and initial servicing of which Italians were recruited. Dutch as well as British officers and seamen helped man the Baltic sailing fleet until sufficient numbers of Russians could be recruited and trained, a situation that was not unusual at the time. Owing to the rapid growth of state navies in early modern Europe, seamen were in relatively short supply, so that hiring foreigners was a standard recourse especially in France and the Netherlands. Between the 1650s and the 1720s, for instance, from 40 to 60 percent of the crews on Dutch ships were not Dutch (they were mainly Danes, Norwegians, and Germans), nor were up to 30 percent of the officers. Similarly, the Swedish naval buildup after 1650 was supported by "a substantial influx of Dutch naval officers, a part of the large-scale immigration of foreigners with special skills which accompanied Sweden's rise as a great power."[16] If Russian practice under Peter was any different in this regard, it was so mainly because of the size of his naval program and the speed with which it was implemented.

The Anglo-Russian naval connection established by Peter was accompanied by a rapid growth of the seaborne Anglo-Russian trade, which continued to be managed largely by the Muscovy, now Russia Company headquartered in London. In 1723 the company transferred its Russian offices and residences from Archangel and Moscow to St. Petersburg. Exported from Russia were the staples of Baltic commerce—grain, timber, hemp, flax, pitch, tar, iron—as well as whale oil, potash, wax, tallow, and caviar, while imported from Britain were manufactured and luxury goods such as textiles, spices, paper, sugar, buttons, eyeglasses, tools, utensils, and instruments of various kinds, glass, clothes, tableware, tobacco, and wine. The trade was carried almost entirely in British ships, necessitating a large resident British colony in St. Petersburg. Britain's primacy in Russian foreign trade for the rest of the eighteenth century has been amply demonstrated by economic historians. They have also shown that from Peter's time until the end of the eighteenth century Russia's overall foreign trade increased in real terms approximately fifteen-fold, and that St. Petersburg quickly became both the largest Russian port and the most important center of this burgeoning international commerce.[17]

It has been calculated that some 1,260 seagoing vessels were built in Russian yards between 1688 and 1725 for fleets launched successively on the White Sea, the Sea of Azov (with access to the Black Sea), the Baltic, and the Caspian (supporting Peter's Persian campaign of 1722–1723).[18] By almost any measure this must count as an outstanding achievement of Peter's reign. Naval support proved decisive in the successful siege of Nöteborg in 1702 (Fig. 10) and in the eventual defeat of Sweden in the long Northern War, which included not only the celebrated naval victory off Hangö Head, Finland, in 1714 but also the little noticed repulse of a Swedish attack on Archangel in 1701 and the diplomatically crucial destruction of a Swedish squadron in 1720. In 1700, at the beginning of the Northern War, the majority of seamen in the infant Russian navy were foreign; in 1721, at the war's end, it was manned by some 7,215 native-born sailors. The Baltic fleet in particular, the largest of the fleets and long thereafter the most important component of the Russian navy, provided vital security for St. Petersburg in its immensely important role as Russia's "window on Europe." According to a British officer who had served in it for eight long years, the Baltic fleet in 1724 comprised 29 seaworthy warships of 36 to 90 guns, a total that gave Russia naval supremacy over Sweden (24 such warships) and Denmark (25). Never generous in his praise, indeed frequently critical of Russian efforts to build up the fleet, this officer still had to allow that "few if any ships in the world are able to wrong the Russian, especially those built at St. Petersburg, if well manned, in the qualification of excellent sailing; and they are incomparably provided with masts, sails, anchors, cables, and cordage, all the proper product of Russia."[19]

Peter's creation of the Russian navy has rightly been called the "Petrine naval revolution."[20] Its future was assured not only by the continual operations of the fleets themselves, especially the Baltic fleet, but by the St. Petersburg Naval Academy. This institution was the first center of higher technical education founded in Russia and, for about ten years, until Peter's Academy of Sciences opened its doors, the first Russian center of modern scientific research. With its British traditions and resident British instructors, the Naval Academy also became a stronghold of English in Russia: the first English grammars for Russians and the first English-Russian dictionaries were published by its press in 1766,

1772, and 1784. The Academy—later also known as the Naval Cadet Corps and the Naval School—remained the principal training site for officers of the Imperial Russian Navy down to 1917, from which time a senior naval staff school, named after Peter the Great, has been located on its premises.

The Naval Academy and its preparatory schools were administratively subordinate to the Admiralty Peter founded first to build ships for the navy and then to run it as well. This famous Petrine institution began life in Voronezh in 1696, was moved to Moscow in 1698, and later, in 1707, to St. Petersburg. Like its very name (Admiralteistvo), it was modeled mainly on the cognate Dutch institution (the Admiraliteit) in Amsterdam. Yet it quickly took on a life and character of its own. From 1709 the Admiralty's primary responsibility was to provide ships for the Baltic fleet, for which scaffolds and slips were constructed in St. Petersburg along with roperies or rigging sheds, mast, sail, and caulking shops, barracks for naval personnel and huts for workers, these soon followed by an Admiralty church and by houses for its leading officials. It was also decided early on that the St. Petersburg Admiralty should be fortified with ramparts, guns, and ditches so as to serve as one of the city's main defenseworks. The result was that by 1718 the Admiralty complex centering on its shipyard constituted one of the five main administrative districts of the new capital, a city within a city and easily the dominant institution, apart from the Baltic fleet itself, of the entire Russian naval establishment. With its thousands of workers and staff (between 1712 and 1721 an estimated 50,000 to 60,000 workers passed through its yard), its outlying forests and sawmills, copper works, iron works, and linen factories (for sailcloth), it had become the single largest industrial enterprise in Russia as well, a status that it retained for the rest of the eighteenth century.

Late in 1717, as Peter began to apply the collegial principle to his central government, he announced that an "Admiralty College" was to be among the new administrative organs shortly to be founded. Run by a board of senior naval officials, the Admiralty College assumed control in 1718 of all existing naval forces and related offices with their ships and dependent shipyards, shops, schools, hospitals, churches, harbors, fortifications, residences, and industrial enterprises, whether located in St. Petersburg or anywhere else in the Russian Empire. The Admiralty College became responsible, in brief, for all aspects of the Imperial Russian navy's administration and economic life. And so it remained until 1802, when in connection with another reorganization of the central government it was transformed into the Ministry of the Navy, an institution that continues in one form or another to this day.

The memory of the Petrine naval revolution has also been perpetuated in the shrine of the *botik* ("little boat") that was discovered by the teen-age Peter at the royal estate of Izmailovo near Moscow in 1688. The boat apparently was built in the 1640s in England, or in Russia by Dutch craftsmen following an "English-type" design.[21] It measures seven meters in length by two in width, is single-masted and shallow-drafted, and is steered by a tiller connected to a large rudder attached to the sternpost: a type common in maritime Europe since late medieval times. Following his inaugural sailing lessons in the boat on waters near Moscow, Peter had stored it for safekeeping in the Kremlin (1701), evincing even then a special regard for it. Years later we find reference to the *botik* in his draft preface to the *Naval Statute,* as noted above. Indeed, in the published version of the preface Peter's editor, Feofan Prokopovich, declared that "the *botik* thus served him [Peter] not only as a childhood pastime, but became the cause of his building a navy, as we now see with wonder." Prokopovich again evoked the *botik* in a "Sermon in Praise of the Russian Fleet" preached before Peter and his entourage in September 1720. In that speech he asserted that it was "to the navy what the seed is to the tree," and more: "from this seed grew a great, wondrous, winged, armored forest of trees." Prokopovich went on to exclaim: "O *botik,* worthy to be gilded! Some have looked diligently for the planks of

Noah's ark in the mountains of Ararat; my advice would be to guard this *botik* and to treasure it as an unforgettable memorial unto the last generation."[22] The advice proved most welcome.

In Moscow early in 1722 Peter ordered the *botik* put on display in the Kremlin in celebration of the recent Peace of Nystad. He then ordered it transported to the Alexander-Nevsky monastery in St. Petersburg, which he had founded in 1721 to commemorate Russia's medieval warrior-saint and his victory, on the ice of the nearby Neva, over invading German and Swedish forces (thus setting a precedent, supposedly, for Peter's victory over Sweden). On May 30, 1723, his birthday, Peter sailed the *botik* down the Neva in a convoy of yachts, barges, and other sailboats to the Admiralty, where it received artillery salutes from ships of the Baltic fleet and from the Peter-Paul fortress. In August 1723 a grand regatta of the Baltic fleet was organized and this time Peter, crossing over to the base at Kronshtadt from St. Petersburg in his *botik* accompanied by a flotilla of more than a hundred other vessels, steered her between the massed ships of the line, all with flags flying, to receive their salute—a rolling fusillade fired from a thousand guns. The *botik* was then installed in the Peter-Paul fortress on a plinth inscribed, "From the amusement of the child came the triumph of the man." On August 30, 1724, the third anniversary of the Peace of Nystad, the *botik* joined the ceremonies at the Alexander-Nevsky monastery marking the deposition of the saint's relics in the monastery's church of the Annunciation. Peter ordered that on August 30 of every year thereafter the *botik* be rowed or sailed upriver to the monastery to commemorate these events.

Thus was solidified the legend of the "grandad [*dedushka*] of the Russian navy," as Peter himself had dubbed the now carefully preserved *botik*. Succeeding Russian monarchs, claiming his mantle, pressed the *botik* into service on various state occasions. Thus at the wedding in 1745 of Grand Duke Peter (grandson of Peter I and the future Peter III) and Grand Duchess Catherine (the future Catherine II), the *botik* appeared in a regatta on the Neva escorted by the reigning Empress Elizabeth (Peter I's daughter) dressed in a naval uniform. Early in her own reign—1760s—Catherine II had a pavilion built next to the church in the Peter-Paul fortress to house the vessel. It soon became a major tourist attraction. More impressively still, in conjunction with the celebrations of the bicentenary of Peter I's birth in 1872, the *botik* was brought back to Moscow in a cortege led by the reigning emperor's brother, where it was greeted by a 101-gun salute and the plaudits of an excited public. It was then put on display at the great Moscow fair of that year, where Russians saw it, a recent investigator suggests, as a symbol of the navy that had "elevated Russia to Great Power status." In the words of a contemporary Russian educator, "The little boat at the head of a gigantic navy—that is the best manifestation of Peter's work and of the advice he gave us in our struggle for success."[23] During the early Soviet era—1920s and 1930s—the shrine of the *botik* was downgraded along with most memorials of the Imperial period, as attested by the absence of any reference to it in the standard guidebooks to what was now called Leningrad. But with the outbreak of World War II and the partial, patriotic rehabilitation of Peter the Great, conqueror of "Germans" and founder of the Russian, now Soviet, navy, his *botik* resurfaced and was prominently installed in the newly created Central Naval Museum housed in the former St. Petersburg Bourse (Birzha) or Stock Exchange. It was there to inspire Russians during the tercentenary of Peter's birth in 1972, and remains so today, while the Soviet Union has come and gone and Peter's city has resumed its original name.

The story of the "grandad of the Russian navy" embalmed in the *botik* is easily grasped, and moralized. In 1997 the *botik* left Russia for the first time and traveled to New York, to become the main attraction of an exhibition on St. Petersburg mounted at the World Trade Center. A reporter for the *New York Times* was fascinated by the comments of visiting or resident Russians, both intellectuals and more ordinary folk. "It mesmerizes me," said one; "Without this boat," said another, "St. Petersburg wouldn't exist." "I touched the wood and it was kind of an electric feeling," said a third; "This was always the least official of our official symbols, something for which we could sincerely express our patriotic feelings." A Russian whose business involved frequent trips between Russia and the United States was also quoted: "The boat symbolizes Peter the Great's attempt to break through Russia's backwardness and isolation and reach out to the West. Peter represents the promise that was never fulfilled."[24]

The shrine of the *botik* remains an essential element of the cult of Peter the Great established in Russia late in his own reign, a cult that shows no signs of withering away—indeed, that in recent years has been newly reinvigorated. The first major monument to the pre-Soviet past erected in post-Soviet Moscow is a gigantic sculpture of Peter, some fifteen stories high. It depicts him as the founder of the Russian navy, standing tall at the helm of a tall ship mounted on a huge pedestal studded with nautical motifs.[25] Whatever one may think of the monument (its size and design are controversial), it does serve to remind us that it was the navy, one way or another, that brought Peter, and then Russia, into Europe and the modern world.

3

Diplomatic and
Bureaucratic Revolutions

The military revolution that took place in early modern Europe was largely driven by dynastic aggrandizement. By this term we mean the relentless pursuit of territorial expansion by hereditary rulers seeking economic gain and strategic security against the similar pretensions of their neighbors. Such rulers regarded the state or governing apparatus over which they presided, and which in some sense they thought they actually owned, as "sovereign," that is, as independent of the control of any other ruler and a law unto itself.

This system of sovereign states—principalities, dukedoms, and kingdoms—first emerged on the Italian peninsula in the fourteenth and fifteenth centuries, with the steady breakdown there of the universal political claims of the Holy Roman Emperor backed by the pope of Rome. Italy had become too densely populated, too rich, too urban, and too culturally diverse to support such claims any longer, especially when the emperor was a German residing somewhere across the Alps and the pope was increasingly seen as a purely spiritual leader with whom one could disagree. The secular, humanistic tendencies of the Italian Renaissance, its passion for civil law and public oratory and naturalistic imagery, only strengthened these developments. And as similar demographic, economic, social, and cultural factors came into play north of the Alps, the Italian system of sovereign states gradually spread, in the sixteenth and seventeenth centuries, to the rest of Europe.

The birth of the modern European state was a revolutionary advance in the history of Europe, and eventually the world, by any standard. An important collaborative study of this huge subject lists four characteristics of the "sovereign state" that became dominant in Europe after 1500: (1) the new state controlled a continuous territory whose borders were relatively well defined; (2) its administration was relatively centralized; (3) it was differentiated from, and its jurisdiction superior to, any other organizations—churches, businesses, family or clan networks, or armies—that were located on the same territory; and (4) it fortified its claims by steadily strengthening its monopoly of the means of physical coercion within its territory. A "modern state" was, and is, "an organization employing specialized personnel which controls a consolidated territory and is recognized as autonomous and integral by the agents of other states." In other words, the rise of modern diplomacy, meaning the system of resident ambassadors, diplomatic immunity, and periodic peace conferences that we now take for granted, was also closely connected with the emergence of the modern state. It too originated in Renaissance Italy and constituted, in its own right, a diplomatic revolution in the history of Europe and eventually the world.[1]

Most modern historians emphasize that in early modern Europe, to quote Charles Tilly, "war made the state, and the state made war." As Tilly explains it:

The building of an effective military machine imposed a heavy burden on the population involved: taxes, conscription, requisitions, and more. The very act of building it—when it worked—produced arrangements which could deliver resources to the government for other purposes. (Thus almost all the major European taxes began as "extraordinary levies" earmarked for particular wars, and became routine sources of government revenue.) The military machine produced the means of enforcing the government's will over stiff resistance: the army. It tended, indeed, to promote territorial consolidation, centralization, differentiation of the instruments of government, and monopolization of the means of coercion, all the fundamental state-making processes.

The point deserves emphasis:

> The formation of standing armies provided the largest single incentive to extraction [of resources from subject populations] and the largest single means of state coercion over the long run of European state-making. Recurrently we find a chain of causation running from (1) change or expansion in land armies to (2) new efforts to extract resources from the subject population to (3) the development of new bureaucracies and administrative innovations to (4) resistance from the subject population to (5) durable increases in the bulk or extractiveness of the state . . . Preparation for war has been the great state-building activity.

At the international level, moreover, wars and their settlement were the "greatest shapers of the European state system as a whole." Beginning with the Peace of Westphalia ending the Thirty Years War (1648), the major modern war settlements produced "incomparably greater alignments of the identities, relations, and relative strengths of European states than any long periods of incremental change between them . . . War shaped, and reshaped, the European state system."[2]

It is sometimes difficult for us today to grasp the centrality of war in the making of modern European history. But it is on the "bureaucratization of war" or the "bureaucratic revolution in warfare," as historians are now calling it, that we shall focus here. The standard work on the subject was done by the famous German sociologist Max Weber, who conceived of bureaucracy as an integral part of a modern or "rational-legal"—as distinct from either a "traditional" or a "transitional"—political system. The crucial characteristics of bureaucracy, in Weber's widely accepted view, include the apportioning of specialized, highly differentiated roles to its members; their recruitment on the basis of educational achievement, usually measured by examination, rather than of birth or social rank; their placement, transfer, and promotion according to universally applicable, not merely local or particular, criteria; and their self-identification as administrators who are salaried professionals and view their work as a career. The practice of decision-making by such administrators within a rational and readily understood context of hierarchy, responsibility, and discipline, said Weber, is also a crucial characteristic of modern bureaucracy.[3]

Weber did not, of course, suppose that functioning bureaucracies always conformed in every respect to his "ideal type"; nor do historians studying the bureaucratic revolution in early modern Europe suppose any such thing. Noble birth and good social connections could facilitate a bureaucratic career in Europe well into the twentieth century. Even in the army it was still much easier for aristocrats than for ordinary folk to reach the higher levels of command, various kinds of patronage were common, and officers' commissions were often for sale. Yet most military officers in early modern Europe, like most civil servants, were becoming career professionals, loyal to the state that hired, often trained, and paid them. Their promotions within a formal chain of command depended more and more on merit or seniority, not social status; and the equipment, regulations, and tactics of the armies in which they served were being standardized. Most important, the armies themselves were assuming a permanent character—institutions of the state as firmly founded as the state itself.

This is the background against which Peter's massive reorganization of the Russian state, and his struggle to join the European state system, should be seen. Peter brought the bureaucratic revolution of early modern Europe to Russia together with the closely connected diplomatic revolution. Both actions were inseparable from the preparation and conduct of his wars, particularly the war with Sweden, which lasted, as we know, for more than twenty years. And both were grounded in his growing realization that by contemporary European standards, especially war-making standards, Muscovite political values and practices were seriously deficient.

Indeed, the state that Peter inherited has been seen by historians as an amalgam of monarchical, dynastic, patrimonial, and theocratic elements, an amalgam that itself warns us against classifying the Muscovite polity as modern according to the criteria outlined above. The Muscovite ruler of pre-Petrine times, even the young Peter, regarded himself, and seems to have been regarded by his subjects, as the residual owner by hereditary right of the entire country—his patrimony—and all its resources, both human and material. He was simultaneously considered a kind of high priest, custodian of the one Orthodox church to which all Russians supposedly belonged and whose "mysteries" or sacraments alone gave them access to the kingdom of heaven. The Muscovite tsardom, in this typically medieval view, was God's kingdom on earth and the tsar, God's earthly viceroy (Fig. 11). "The sovereign was at the center of a theocratic vision of government," as one historian puts it, or again, in the words of another: "The image of a Russian Orthodox community served a unifying function in Muscovy and in significant measure determined the outlines of Muscovite political culture."[4] In two large painted depictions of the tsar dating to the 1670s and 1680s—one of Peter's father, Tsar Aleksei, the other of his elder half-brother, Tsar Fedor—the subject is arrayed in sacerdotal dress and the image itself is in the style of a holy icon. These are not the secular rulers depicted in the naturalistic portraits that became standard in post-Renaissance Europe and then under Peter in Russia. They are, rather, old-fashioned royal saints.[5]

The power that Peter inherited was vested in the tsar-father, his family, and a court composed of several hundred grandees (boyars) and senior noble servitors. All of them lived with their families and numerous dependents in and around the citadel (kremlin) of Moscow except when the men were serving as governors in the provinces, leading the army on campaign, conducting missions abroad, trading in Archangel or Astrakhan, or running ironworks in the Tula region or saltworks in the Urals. This establishment was paralleled by the much smaller court of the Moscow patriarch, the senior bishop of the Russian Orthodox church. Indeed, the patriarch's constant ceremonial presence, pretensions to co-sovereignty, and network of subordinate bishoprics and monasteries evoked an aura of theocracy. Apart from a hodgepodge of semi-feudal, semi-regular armed forces, the tsar's power was exercised in and through the boyars' council and a welter of some eighty or more central offices whose overlapping functions varied enormously in territorial as well as administrative or judicial scope: they definitely were not the clearly demarcated, formally coordinated governmental departments called for by theorists of the modern state. The officials and staffs of these offices, semi-professional at best by modern standards, together with their sparsely distributed provincial counterparts, attempted to govern in some rudimentary fashion—to extract resources from—a vast realm of subordinate tsardoms and principalities. These in turn were composed mainly of landed estates controlled by court, ecclesiastical, and gentry servitors and worked by peasant families, the latter living under *krepostnoe pravo*, or the law of bonded servitude (serfdom). The prevalence of serfdom alone, the basic socio-economic condition of the great majority of the tsar's subjects, has been taken by historians as a major marker of Muscovy's "medieval" or pre-modern character. So has its comparatively paltry urban network, which in the later seventeenth century, with respect to population aggregates and the level of its administrative and commercial development, resembled China's in the late fourteenth century or those of Japan, France, England, Italy, Germany, or the Netherlands in the late fifteenth or early sixteenth centuries.[6]

By contemporary European standards, in other words, we seem to have something of an anomaly here: a decidedly medieval society and economy dominated by a proto-modern or semi-modern state. The anomaly is fully reflected in the main legal document produced by this state, the so-called *Ulozhenie* promulgated by Tsar Aleksei in 1649. This document is in many respects both a civil code, regulating property matters and private disputes in great detail, and a criminal code, prescribing variously harsh punishments for violating the tsar's laws. But it also prescribes the tax-paying, rental, and service obligations along with the residential restrictions imposed by the tsar on ordinary townsfolk and peasants. In addition, it affirms the property rights granted by him to the landholding elite in return for military service, above all their right to have peasants bound in perpetuity to their lands (the essence of serfdom). The *Ulozhenie* of 1649, in short, is not a rationalized, regularized, Roman-inspired legal compilation of the sort being published in contemporary Europe and later thought typical of "modern juridical thought."[7] Although it does describe a highly centralized governmental apparatus embodied in the "Sovereign Tsar and Autocrat of all Russia," the *constitution* of this state, its lineaments or salient features, its origins or legal basis, its component parts, its justification for being, are nowhere defined. In fact, it may fairly be said that the Muscovite state, its ramshackle law code notwithstanding, was in essence the kind of patrimonial and feudal state that predominated in Europe from the end of the Roman Empire until the advent of the Renaissance.

Peter moved decisively both to make the state he inherited function more efficiently and to justify it legally in terms compatible with, indeed borrowed from, contemporary European sources. The prolonged succession crisis, punctuated by murderous coups, in which he assumed power only made such moves all the more imperative. His solution to the crisis, and to Russia's comparative political backwardness, was to bring to Russian government the bureaucratic revolution of seventeenth-century Europe as it had been implemented by absolute monarchies in Prussia, certain other German states, and Sweden and codified in the doctrines of cameralism (from Latin *camera,* "chamber, bureau." Cameralism taught that the object of government was to increase the state's revenues by a corresponding expansion of its capacity to regulate society and the economy.). There is space here only to mention the more salient features of Peter's bureaucratic revolution. We will also largely ignore, for the same reason, its underlying politics: the endless peculation, intrigue, and jockeying for official position and royal favor among the ruling elite, many of whom Peter had inherited along with his throne but many of whom, like Alexander Menshikov, he himself had empowered. The endless politics no doubt affected the pace and even degree of governmental reform under Peter, but not its essential outlines.[8]

The more salient features of Peter's bureaucratic revolution include the establishment, with his military and naval statutes serving as models, of a comprehensive system of state-service ranking based on seniority and merit (achievement) rather than kinship or custom (ascription), all as provided by his famous Table of Ranks of January 1722 and related measures. They also include his creation from 1718 on of a new state administrative apparatus whose procedures were codified in a detailed *General Regulation* promulgated in January 1720. The new apparatus consisted, at the center, of newly amalgamated and functionally defined executive agencies (the Colleges of War, Foreign Affairs, Justice, Commerce, Admiralty, and so forth), each headed by a board of officials rather than a single minister and all coordinated and controlled by the Senate (founded in 1711) assisted by a regime of procurators and subordinate "fiscals" *(fiskaly)*. The latter's duties combined those of fiscal inspectors with others more typical of judicial prosecutors, and they were supposed to ensure honest and efficient administration at every level of the government. The elimination of what was increasingly seen as governmental corruption rather than business as usual, the eradication especially of the bribery and embezzlement that had been characteristic of both previous Muscovite governance and his own regime, had emerged as a principal motive of Peter's reform of the state. All senior officials—senators and members of the governing colleges (each consisting of a president, vice-president, four assessors, and four councilors)—were to be appointed by the monarch after nomination and careful vetting by the Senate or respective college: no incompetents, even if they were relatives or old cronies, were to be considered.

Peter's bureaucratic revolution also encompassed the Russian Orthodox church, whose traditional head office, the Moscow patriarchate, was replaced in 1721 by a college of the monarch's clerical appointees dubbed the Holy Synod and assisted by a Senate-like bureaucracy under its own chief procurator. The patriarchal throne had been left vacant since 1700, when Adrian, its last incumbent, died and Peter declined to permit the election of a successor. By creating the Holy Synod to replace it he had incorporated the administration and revenues of the church into those of his reformed state. "Secularization" in this quite specific sense of the term, meaning significant institutional and legal enlargement of the state's wealth and authority at the expense of those of the church, and the political subordination of the latter to the former, has long been regarded as a major aspect of political modernization.[9]

Other notable instances of Peter's bureaucratic revolution are his foundation in 1724 of the tax-supported St. Petersburg Academy of Sciences, whose responsibilities included training officials for state service, publishing books needed by the government, mapping the whole of Russia (for the first time), and conducting state-sponsored research. The Academy was to be run, according to its Imperial charter, by officials appointed by the ruler, who was always to be its patron. Peter also used bureaucratic means to clamp an unprecedented degree of central-government control over the economic and social life of his country, especially by instituting the head tax, which was to be collected annually from every male "soul" in the country (except nobles and clergy) and was initially administered by the army. The web of fiscal inspectors charged with enforcing the laws and rooting out corruption further enhanced government control of society and the economy, as did the number of bureaucrats staffing the central and provincial offices, which more than doubled. And to justify it all Peter adopted a secular, imperialist ideology of monarchical absolutism that was given expression in a series of verbal texts printed on newly founded presses in a new "civil" type—two such texts will be looked at shortly—as well as in a huge array of new visual forms, the latter including printed and painted official portraits, medals, coins, maps, flags, seals, and coats-of-arms.[10]

One of Peter's governmental reforms, his decree of February 1722 regulating the succession to the throne, exceeded the reach of even the most absolutist of contemporary European monarchies. According to the decree, the succession was to be by appointment of the reigning monarch rather than by right of inheritance, the practice prevailing before Peter in Muscovy as well as in most of Europe. In fact, by Peter's decree the reigning monarch could disinherit an unworthy child (as he himself had done, in the case of Tsarevich Aleksei) and adopt as successor whomever he, or indeed she, chose. His law opened the way for women to reign in Russia for sixty-six of the remaining (after his death) seventy-five years of the eighteenth century, starting with his own successor, Empress Catherine I. Empress Catherine II (1762–1796), arguably the most successful of his successors, also had, like Catherine I, only a marital connection with the Romanov dynasty. It was her son,

Emperor Paul (1796–1801), resentful of his mother's long reign, who established the succession thereafter by strict male primogeniture, a move that arguably did nothing to improve the quality of the monarch sitting on the Russian throne but did stabilize the new ruler's accession (except in the case of Paul's son, Alexander I, who died in 1825 leaving no sons, thus precipitating a crisis).

We might also note, among major initiatives to reform (reform) his state, Peter's efforts to establish a comprehensive new judicial code based on current European models which would supplant the ramshackle *Ulozhenie* of 1649. It is true that those efforts failed (as did analogous attempts under successive monarchs until the reign of Nicholas I, more than a century later): a draft code was completed in Peter's time but never promulgated, remaining in the archives to encourage future legislators. Nor did Peter succeed in separating judicial process from government administration, an idea that was contrary to Muscovite traditions and would not be fully implemented in Russia until the Judicial Reform of 1864. Nor did his efforts to induce a measure of urban and provincial self-government in Russia along contemporary German or Swedish lines meet with more than limited success, running contrary as they did to ingrained Muscovite habits of deferring to the tsar and his agents. But none of these outcomes, like the related failure—no surprise—to eradicate governmental corruption, can alter the fact that the modern Russian state, in its bureaucratic, military, legal, and ideological essence, dates to Peter the Great.

What kind of polity was the Petrine state? A "well-ordered police state" of the type emerging in the contemporary German lands is the most considered descriptor so far devised. As one historian says, by "energetically and systematically" adopting the "concepts and practices of the well-ordered police state" of early modern Europe, particularly Germany, the Petrine governmental structure gradually if unevenly attained a "coherence of form that provided a framework for all of Peter's other innovative enterprises as well as the institutional basis of the Imperial regime throughout the remainder of its existence [to 1917]."[11] ("Police" in this formulation refers to a government's efforts to "polish" or civilize its subjects through education, better health care, and so on, not simply to its efforts to suppress crime.) Another close student of Peter's reforms has proposed that what emerged from them was a "modernized service state," meaning one still characterized by a "universal regime of services and exactions" but marked now by "the transition from personal to bureaucratic rule." Yet "taken as a whole," this student concludes, "the Petrine system of domestic administration in its final, albeit unfinished, form comes closer to the modern police state or a military dictatorship" than to the early modern idea of the well-regulated police state.[12] A third answer to the question suggests that Peter only "partially dismantled" the "patrimonial state" he inherited from his Muscovite predecessors, with ominous consequences for the future; another, that his state was simply the traditional Muscovite "autocracy" in a newly militarized and bureaucratized form.[13]

There is some truth in all these evaluations, to be sure. But if we look at Peter's reformed state as much in its contemporary European as in its traditional Russian context, it might be best described as an "absolute monarchy" of the type emerging (or already emerged) in contemporary France, Prussia, or Sweden, all notable for their somewhat variable mix of secular, dynastic, militarist, bureaucratic, juristic, and personal features. Such hereditary monarchies all made use of newly modernized armed forces and state bureaucracies to enforce their rule at home and promote their claims abroad; all claimed full sovereignty over their subjects and personally directed their governments; all were concerned to govern in accordance with clear, detailed, enlightened laws ("enlightened" because they were clear and detailed and ultimately based on natural law); and all justified their assumption of supreme authority or "absolute" power over any other jurisdictions on their territory—law courts, churches, feudal lords, city councils—less in religious terms than in terms of the common good, or the good of the state itself. This was the modern European state in its absolutist, early modern form. Only a minority of states in early modern Europe were constitutional monarchies or republics, the latter dominated by patrician or aristocratic oligarchies. By far the majority of contemporary European states were absolute monarchies and they, it is hardly surprising, were Peter's model—particularly that established in neighboring Sweden, long Russia's rival in the Baltic region.[14] Seen in this context, Peter's new state was a Russian variant of a common European type and arguably as successful, in its time and place, as the others were in theirs. In the terms deployed by the Petrine regime itself, Russia was now much more than the Orthodox Christian community and royal patrimony of old centered in semi-Asiatic Moscow. It was a European "empire" of all its Christian subjects—Orthodox, Lutheran, Roman Catholic—headquartered in St. Petersburg, a state that even the monarch himself, though legally absolute (sovereign) in his power, was morally bound to serve for the common good.

Peter's government published two major political treatises—the first of their kind in Russia—to justify the new state. One is entitled *The Right* [or *Legitimacy*] *of the Monarch's Will in Designating the Heir to His/Her Realm (Pravda voli monarshei vo opredelenii naslednika derzhavy svoei)* and was first published in Moscow in 1722 in both the traditional Cyrillic and the new civil type, the latter in an exceptionally large edition of 1,200 copies. It was edited and at least partly written by Feofan Prokopovich, the Ukrainian ecclesiastic who had arrived in St. Petersburg in 1716 to become Peter's principal advisor on church affairs and leading public defender.[15] A second edition was printed in both Moscow and St. Petersburg, in the civil type only, in 1726—in an astonishing total of nearly 20,000 copies—and a German edition was printed in Berlin in 1724. Peter obviously attached great importance to the *Pravda,* whose ostensible purpose was to explain, and defend, the radically new succession law of 1722 but whose more general aim was to trumpet the new doctrine of absolute monarchy in Russia. Specialists have studied the treatise carefully, though the same cannot be said for historians generally, who have tended to misunderstand or ignore it.[16]

The main body of the *Pravda* consists of sixteen numbered "Reasons or Arguments" in support of absolute monarchy and the new succession law, many of them subdivided into numbered paragraphs or points, these followed by forty-seven "Examples or Instances" drawn from both "human history" and the Bible to illustrate or affirm these arguments. A few prefatory passages and a kind of afterword complete the text. The first nine of the sixteen Reasons outline the "authority of all parents generally," the last seven, the "authority of sovereign parents," that is, monarchs. Six of the Examples are taken from the Bible, the remaining forty-one from "human history" as recorded by assorted authors, the earliest of them writing at the time of King Cyrus of Persia (as cited in a work by the famous Dutch jurist Hugo Grotius), the most recent in the reign of Grand Prince Ivan III of Moscow (fifteenth century). Several of the biblical passages are bolstered by extended quotations from the Greek and Latin fathers of the early Christian church. It is also notable that the *Pravda* was written not in the ornate Church Slavonic language favored by the clergy but in a simpler style that freely borrowed terms from western European languages, primarily German and Latin.

In other words, the new doctrine of absolute monarchy was defended in the *Pravda* first by reference to a set of religious texts long revered in both Christian East and West, which was to be expected, given the treatise's clerical author or authors. But these "reasons" and their supporting "examples" had not been deployed before in Russia, in a language that was more or less readily accessible to literate lay Russians and in defense of monarchical absolutism. Moreover, the *Pravda* also deployed arguments drawn from the natural-law theorists of early modern Europe, most notably, as just mentioned, Hugo Grotius. For instance, the treatise at one point invites its Russian readers to consider "what signifies the glorious royal title, *majesty* [*velichestvo*], or, as other European peoples say from Latin, *maestat* or *maestet?*" An explanation promptly follows:

> This word simply means, in grammatical usage, any kind of precedence of one thing over another . . . But we are considering *majesty* here not in this spacious sense, but only in that of political philosophy . . . wherefore in general, among all the peoples whether Slavic or other, this word *maestet* or *velichestvo* is used for the very highest precedent honor, and is given to the supreme authority alone, and signifies not only their transcendent dignity, than which, after God's, there is none greater in the world, but also [their] supreme lawgiving, executive, and judicial authority, undeniable and itself not subject to any laws whatsoever. Thus the most distinguished law teachers describe *majesty,* among whom Hugo Grotius says as follows: *The highest authority (called majesty) is that whose actions are not subject to another authority, such that they could be annulled by the will of another; and when I say another, I exclude him who has such supreme authority: for him it is possible to change his will. (Hugo, On the Law of War and Peace, book 1, chapter 3, number 7).*

Furthermore, the *Pravda* continues,

> it must be understood that when the teachers of law say that the highest authority, called *majesty,* is not subject to any other authority, they speak only about human authority; it is subject to divine authority and the laws of God, whether those written in human hearts or in the Ten Commandments . . . But in being subject to divine law, it is liable for transgression thereof only to God, not to human judg-

ment . . . We know this, first, from natural reason: since this authority is called, and is, the supreme, highest, and ultimate, how can it be subject to human laws? If it were subject, it would not be supreme. And when sovereigns themselves do what civil statutes command, they do so by will, not by need: so that by their example they inspire subjects to willing observance of the law, or they affirm that the laws are good and beneficial.[17]

Numerous quotations from Scripture and the early church fathers are then adduced, all leading to the conclusion that an absolute monarch "is fully empowered and free" to designate his own successor.

The *Pravda* or *Right of the Monarch's Will*, composed by Prokopovich and others by order of Peter, thus exhibits a distinctly modern, or early modern, political outlook. Indeed, it has been fairly compared to a tract by Bishop Bossuet published in 1709 similarly defending the absolute monarchy of Louis XIV of France and especially to *The True Law of Free Monarchies* (1598) attributed to King James I of England. It is also remarkable for the geographical as well as intellectual expansion of horizons its text represents. Its reference to the Russians as among "other European peoples," for example, was a novelty in Russia, the word "Europe" itself—*Evropa*—being a neologism fixed in written Russian by means of this and other Petrine texts. Elsewhere the *Pravda* invokes the wider European world to which Russia rightly aspires to belong, as in this passage:

Innumerable so to speak are the books composed by many authors on civil statutes and laws, and nowhere in them is any doubt raised as to whether a parent can deprive a son of his inheritance: and so the whole civilized world is our witness to this. And should someone doubt that there are so many teachers and lawmakers, then one can show him even here in Russia, and especially in royal St. Petersburg, up to three hundred and more law books in which are discussed the causes and circumstances of disinheriting unworthy sons; and what more [might be found] should we enter the famous and great libraries all over Europe![18]

And then there are the many illustrative examples from European history presented in the *Pravda* to support its central arguments. Locating Russia in Europe, here verbally, at other times by means of imagery or architecture (see Chapter 4), was the overall goal, it bears repeating, of the entire Petrine project.

The other major political treatise produced by Peter's regime was entitled, in its contemporary English translation, *A Discourse Concerning the Just* [Legal] *Reasons Which his Czarish Majesty, Peter I . . . had for beginning the War against the King of Sweden, Charles XII, Anno 1700*. This treatise by Peter Shafirov, a leading diplomat of the Petrine regime whom we met in Chapter 1, was first printed in St. Petersburg in the civil type in 1717 and again in Moscow in 1719, in St. Petersburg in 1722, and in a contemporary German edition (from which the English translation, first published in 1723, was taken); and it too was published in what was for the time an enormous number of copies, a total of some 22,000. These details demonstrate, once more, Peter's eagerness to disseminate the treatise's message as widely as possible: the message, in a nutshell, that Russia's long war with Sweden was both necessary and just. Moreover, not only did the *Discourse* articulate for the first time Russian acceptance of the norms of international law as understood in contemporary Europe; it also represented, again for the first time, Russia's formal, public bid for membership in the European state system.[19]

Shafirov's diplomatic career, as noted earlier, had placed him at nearly every crucial juncture of the Northern War. He was a member of Peter's Grand Embassy to Europe of 1697–1698, during which, while passing through Riga, the tsar allegedly suffered an insult from the local Swedish authorities that subsequently became, according to the *Discourse,* a major cause of the war. In 1699 he was among the representatives of Denmark, Poland-Saxony, and Russia who prepared the joint declaration of war against Sweden, and in 1701 he took part in the negotiations between Peter himself and King Augustus II of Poland-Saxony cementing their alliance. In 1703 he became personal secretary to F. A. Golovin, the Muscovite grandee who would assume the new title of chancellor or de facto minister of foreign affairs. On Golovin's death in 1706 and replacement by another grandee, G. I. Golovkin, Shafirov became vice chancellor, a title he formally assumed in 1709 after working diligently behind the scenes in support of Russia's victory over Sweden at Poltava. That same year he was created a baron of the Holy Roman Empire and appointed to distinguished knightly orders by the kings of Poland and Prussia. In 1710 he was created *baron* in Russia by Peter and endowed with country estates.

In the post-Poltava years, as Russia under Peter became steadily more involved in European affairs, Shafirov's diplomatic activity grew apace. High points included negotiating the marriages of Peter's nieces Anna (the future empress) and Catherine with, respectively, the dukes of Courland and Mecklenburg, which took place in 1710 and 1716. In 1717 he accompanied the tsar and Chancellor Golovkin to Paris and Amsterdam, where the conclusion of a Franco-Prussian-Russian trade and political agreement (August 1717) formally recognized Russia's role as a European power (Fig. 12). Shafirov had also spent much of the period 1711–1713 under house arrest in Constantinople as hostage to Russian commitments made after the defeat by Turkish forces at the battle by the Pruth, until a peace treaty with the Ottoman Empire was signed. In 1717 he was named vice-president of the new College of Foreign Affairs; in 1719, a knight of Peter's highly exclusive new Order of St. Andrew; and in 1722, a senator. Shafirov's career, in short, embodies the revolutionary transition in Russian officialdom from the closed world of the Muscovite Ambassadorial

Office (where both he and his father had worked as clerks) to the grand stage of European politics and diplomacy. In his Introduction to the *Discourse* Shafirov refers to himself as a loyal Russian "patriot" moved to defend his sovereign, Tsar Peter, against the calumnies heaped on him by Swedish propaganda. But in so doing he produced what one authority has described as a "legal-historical brief" that is notably "well versed in the theory and practice of early eighteenth-century international law and diplomacy."[20] It certainly was, for a Russian of his day and age, a remarkable achievement.

Equally impressive is the treatise's language, which represents a major lexical and perforce semantic expansion of Russian while promoting the modernization of its grammar and style (a point to which we will return in the following chapter). From its very first page the text of the *Discourse* is studded with new governmental, naval, and military terms as well as with others that are specifically legal or diplomatic in nature. Most of these terms permanently entered the Russian language. And all of them plainly show, along with the phrases and sentences in which they are used, Shafirov's close acquaintance with, even mastery of, contemporary European diplomatic culture.

The *Discourse* is also noteworthy for its affirmation of absolute monarchy—"Great potentates in this world have over them none but the supreme judgment of God"—and for its personal endorsement of Peter's policy of Europeanization. Before his time, we read here, "except for the Russian language none of the Russian people knew how to read and write"; but "now we see even His Majesty himself [Peter] speaking German [or Dutch], and several thousand of his subjects of the Russian nation, male and female, skilled in various European languages, such as Latin, Greek, French, German, Italian, English, and Dutch, and of such conduct moreover that they can be compared without shame to all other European peoples."[21] This statement sums up much of the spirit of Peter's revolution as a whole. Whatever had been Russia's position in the world before his reign it was now, thanks to his reorganization of the army, creation of a navy, victories over Sweden, introduction of the new arts and sciences, and reform of the government, indisputably a European power. And as such it deserved equal treatment from the other European powers.

By the time of Peter's death Russia had become a full member of the European system of sovereign states—itself a diplomatic revolution within the larger revolution that had brought the system into being. Permanent Russian embassies had been established in all the European capitals, this in sharp contrast to the single one that existed, in Warsaw, when Peter came to power. The embassies were staffed not by the robed and bearded Muscovite envoys occasionally sent west by Peter's predecessors, monolingual, ever suspicious of their hosts, and terrified of departing from their rigid instructions, but by fashionably dressed, bewigged and clean-shaven ambassadors, able to negotiate on their own in French, German, or Italian and often accompanied—truly amazing to say—by their comparably equipped spouses (Figs. 13, 14). In fact, one of Peter's most versatile ambassadors, Andrei Matveev (Fig. 14), while doing his duty in London, actually contributed importantly—with Peter's vigorous backing—to the final elaboration in Europe of the law on diplomatic immunity. Matveev had been arrested for debt and thrown into prison. The British government, eager to placate the enraged tsar, not only formally apologized to him and fully compensated his ambassador but pushed a bill through Parliament providing absolute immunity to all "Ambassadors and other Publick Ministers of Foreign princes and States" who had been "authorised and received as such." Other European states soon followed suit.[22] A Russian diplomat representing Peter had thus helped to shape an important component of modern international relations. Moreover, Russian princesses had now married German princes and were living with their spouses in their German states; the Baltic was being transformed from a Swedish into a Russian lake; a Russian garrison guaranteed the independence of Poland; and St. Petersburg, guarded by Peter's Baltic fleet, was fast becoming the capital of northern Europe. The formerly isolated kingdom of Muscovy was no more.

4

Cultural Revolution

$\mathcal{E}$ach of Peter's grand revolutionary projects—his creation of the navy, massive reorganization of the army, bureaucratization of the state, and injection of Russia into Europe—entailed the adoption by Russians of countless new *cultural* practices, values, and norms. How to build and sail a fleet of modern warships; how to uniform, train, equip, provision, deploy, and command in battle a modern military machine; how to organize and operate a new-style bureaucracy; how to conduct diplomacy on equal terms with the *other* European states; and how to rationalize the new governing system in appropriate conceptual terms: all this had to be learned by Russians within a single generation if the new Petrine state, the Russian Empire, the great power now of northern Europe, was to survive the death of its founder.

New ways of dress, deportment, communication, navigation, building, gardening, gunnery, drawing, computing, measuring, sculpting, writing, visualizing, indeed of thinking had to be adopted along with the new vocabularies needed for naming these activities and all the new weapons, tools, and devices associated with them. A cultural revolution thus underlay and ultimately linked up all of Peter's revolutionary projects, "culture" being our common word for the innumerable ways human beings have of making and doing things, and of thinking and talking about them. Language is culture, as are literature, music, painting, sculpture, architecture, and the graphic arts; so are ways of cooking, fighting, dressing, governing, dancing, feasting, praying, courting, and so on. But the meaning of "cultural revolution," a term used rather sparingly by historians, is perhaps less obvious.

The Protestant Reformation, one historian has argued, was not only "a legislative and administrative transaction tidily concluded by a religious settlement in 1559" but a "profound cultural revolution" as well. Another historian has shown how a cultural revolution occurred in conjunction with the political and social changes of the French Revolution of the late eighteenth century. Stalin is said to have launched a cultural revolution in Soviet Russia in 1928–1931 in order to consolidate his dictatorship. And the drastic changes in thinking about the natural world associated with the names of Copernicus, Descartes, Galileo, Newton, and Leibniz, among others, are still called, more than fifty years after the term was coined, the Scientific Revolution of the seventeenth century.[1] It is notable that in each of these very different cases the changes in culture being discussed were major, and recognized as such by contemporaries. They were also consciously intended, at least by an active minority; they happened relatively suddenly, making the post-revolutionary stage readily distinguishable from the pre-revolutionary one; and they produced transformations in their respective societies which were lasting. Indeed, historians everywhere are turning to culture as a more inclusive descriptor of human activity than "politics" or "the economy" or "social relations," all of which retain, of course, a prominent place in historical study. And the major events in history thus construed, the decisive turning points, are called cultural revolutions, which may or may not have occurred in conjunction with political, economic, or social revolutions.

In the case of Russia under Peter, it cannot be said that the changes in either the economy or the society engineered by his regime, mainly in support of the war effort, amounted to an economic or a social revolution. The noble elite was newly regimented by Peter; new tax burdens were imposed on the mostly peasant masses; and both industry and foreign trade underwent a sharp upsurge. But none of these changes resulted in a fundamental reordering of society or the economy. Nor could it be said that a full-scale political revolution—the replacement of one ruling elite by another, or a fundamental change in the very structure of government—took place in Peter's time, although his "bureaucratic revolution," coupled with his massive reorganization of the army, creation of the navy, and achievement for Russia of great-power status in Europe, surely constituted a political revolution in some secondary, less drastic sense of the term. Rather, what happened of greatest historical significance in Russia during Peter's time was a cultural revolution, a revolution that issued from but also transcended all the changes that took place in the political, economic, and social arenas of contemporary Russian life.

Three main aspects of Peter's cultural revolution have been studied in detail—the architectural, the visual, and the verbal. And it has been demonstrated fairly conclusively that the changes which took place in all three respects together constituted a cultural revolution as defined by the criteria adduced above. These changes, in sum, were consciously intended, happened relatively suddenly, were recognized as major by contemporaries, and produced transformations which were lasting. We will look at each set of changes in turn, beginning with those in architecture.[2]

In 1717, during his visit to France, Peter was named an honorary member of the Paris Academy of Sciences, several of whose savants were to help him establish a similar academy in St. Petersburg. The honor was conferred by the Paris Academy in recognition of Peter's military victories over Sweden and Russia's enhanced status in Europe, to be sure, but also in appreciation of his efforts to reform his country in keeping with the values of contemporary

European civilization. The latter theme was revived in the eulogy of Peter given at the Academy in 1725, where among other tributes the speaker declared that he had "transformed the existing architecture, [which was] coarse and deformed in the utmost degree; or rather, he caused architecture to be born in his country."[3] The proposition, startling as it may seem today, was virtually self-evident to educated Europeans of Peter's time and, more important here, to a significant portion of the Russian elite.

When educated people in early modern Europe talked about architecture, they meant the art and science of building edifices in certain clearly defined ways. Such edifices included churches, palaces, and private houses ("civil architecture"); fortifications ("military architecture"); and ships ("naval architecture"). Although the three branches were interrelated to some degree, the first, civil architecture, was considered preeminent by reason of its obviously greater social importance. Civil architecture in Europe was also thought to have gone through three periods or states—the ancient, the gothic (medieval), and the modern—of which the ancient, the architecture of Classical Greece and Rome, was aesthetically and even technically preeminent. The ancients, in this view, had set the standards of architectural beauty and grandeur, which were debased during the gothic Middle Ages and then revived in the Renaissance, thus launching the modern era. There were no two ways about it. Whether it assumed forms that scholars would later classify as Renaissance, Mannerist, Baroque, or Neoclassical, architecture at its reputed best in early modern Europe conformed basically to Classical norms of proportion and decoration, particularly as these were embodied in the five architectural orders: the Doric, Ionic, Corinthian, Tuscan (or Etruscan), and Composite. Each order consisted of a column-and-beam unit regulated by a proportional rule and garnished by a set repertory of ornament and moldings—all as established in sixteenth-century Italy by Sebastiano Serlio, as subsequently popularized by Vignola, and as variously utilized all over Europe in the building of countless palaces, mansions and more ordinary houses, churches both inside and out, tombs, fireplaces, arches, portals, and gardens. It was architecture in this sense that the eulogist of the Paris Academy had in mind when praising Peter for implanting it in Russia.

The process had begun, in fact, with Peter's youthful military and naval exercises. Extensive fortifications had been built in Russia before his time, of course, but they were of a timelessly wooden or earthen variety: timber walls and watchtowers reinforced with palisades of sharpened stakes alternating with long ditches and huge mounds of earth. Sizable brick fortifications began to appear in the late fifteenth century (the kremlin of Moscow), it is true, the best of which were erected under Italian masters in conformity with the norms of medieval European and particularly Italian military architecture. Traditional Muscovite decorative forms— the tent-roof, for example—were soon added, and the structures thereby acquired, in European eyes, an exotic as well as somewhat dated appearance. Muscovite fortifications proved adequate to the task of defending the southern and eastern borders of the country against the incursions of Tatar and other indigenous nomads and plainsmen; they were, however, much less effective on the western front against invading Polish and Swedish forces. By contemporary European standards, in short, Russian military architecture on the eve of Peter's reign was on the whole medieval in quality and rather alien in style (Fig. 15). At best it was, says one expert, "imposing rather than advanced," leaving the country vulnerable to invasion from the west—an ever-present threat during Peter's earlier years on the throne.[4]

"Modern" fortifications in Europe, like modern architecture generally, went back to Renaissance Italy. There builders had responded to the growing range and power of siege artillery by reducing the vulnerable tall towers of the medieval castle to walltop level and by lowering the walls themselves while making them thicker and smoother and setting them in wide, deep ditches.

Triangular or "arrowhead" bastions were pushed out from the walls to permit defending artillery to sweep all approaches to the fortress, which was now pentagonal in plan rather than square or rectangular. The guiding principle was one of horizontal rather than vertical defense, with the bastion rather than the tower playing the key role: the batteries of up to four cannon emplaced in each of the two flanks connecting the bastion's angular head with the wall behind it—the curtain—protected both the curtain itself and the slanting faces of the neighboring bastions. An entire city could be ringed with bastions of the new type to provide a defensive system with no blind spots. Then the space beyond the ditch surrounding the bastioned fortification was invested with a long glacis of tamped earth on which attackers would be exposed to the fortress's cannon, and with numerous outworks covering additional artillery emplacements designed to keep the besiegers even further at bay. Sieges became lengthy, difficult, costly affairs, prompting a corresponding development of siegecraft. Troops and artillery advanced on the fortress under siege in a series of carefully calculated and methodically executed movements protected by earthworks and trenches dug parallel to the fortress and its external defensive lines. These maneuvers in turn spurred the development by fortress commanders of ever more elaborate outworks. In short, the interlocked development of fortification and siegecraft in early modern Europe produced military architecture of an entirely unprecedented size and complexity, relics of which may still be seen all over the European world.

Mini-forts of the modern type were built by foreign officers in Russian service on the royal estates of Preobrazhenskoe and Kolomenskoe near Moscow expressly for young Tsar Peter's war games (Fig. 7). According to General Patrick Gordon, the "play" fort at Kolomenskoe was designed in 1693–1694 by Peter himself, who directed the ensuing mock siege, all in preparation for the campaigns against Azov in 1695 and 1696.[5] The Ottoman fortifications at Azov, probably the most advanced that Peter had yet encountered, were extensively upgraded by hundreds of builders recruited on his orders in Europe after his forces had conquered the town (Fig. 8). Thousands of Russian settlers were brought down to Azov, which was to become a major Russian port and military base named "Petropolis," or "Peter's city." The whole enterprise had to be abandoned after the Russian defeat by the Turks in 1711, and it was not until the reign of Catherine II (1780s) that Russia permanently took control of the northern Black Sea coast including the Crimean peninsula. Yet it was in the Azov campaigns and subsequent building projects that Peter first seriously utilized the techniques of modern siegecraft and fortification, and first faced the problems of modern town planning, experiences he would later put to good use in building his "Petropolis" on the Baltic.

Similarly, it was in connection with the second and successful Azov campaign that Peter first seriously immersed himself in the problems of modern shipbuilding. Again, he and his company had made initial preparations when constructing between 1688 and 1693 their "toy fleet" for sailing on lakes north of Moscow and eventually on the White Sea and the Arctic Ocean. Indeed, General Gordon attributed the victory at Azov to the thoroughness of these preparations, which led to the successful siege of the Turkish citadel by a fleet of galleys and gunboats built at Voronezh, on the Don river, with the help of Dutch shipwrights brought down from Archangel. It was an achievement, as Gordon put it, "thought by many impossible to be brought to perfection . . . in this country."[6] Peter himself later declared, as shown in Chapter 2, that the creation of the Russian navy had begun then and there, at Voronezh and Azov in 1696.

The Petrine revolution in naval architecture, like that in military and then civil architecture, soon came to be centered in and around St. Petersburg, whose foundations were laid in 1703 on ground captured from the Swedes. The first major structures in what became the new capital were the Peter-Paul fortress (Fig. 16), so called after its church of Sts. Peter and Paul, and the Admiralty shipbuilding complex, whose ramparts formed part of the city's first defensive system. These buildings were designed, like the masonry fortress and church that soon replaced their wooden predecessors, by the recently arrived Italian-Swiss architect Dominico (also Domenico) Trezzini. By 1710 a more or less permanent population of 8,000 laborers, soldiers, seamen, and others, together with a seasonal population of that many again and more, were living and working and worshiping in some 16,000 mostly wooden houses, shops, and churches hastily thrown up around the fortress and the Admiralty. The houses included Peter's own *domik,* a simple wooden structure built in a Dutch style he had found to his liking while living in Holland in 1697–1698 (Fig. 17). By 1710, in other words, a rudimentary city had come into being, a city that was to be built entirely in the "new" or "modern" style (in Russian the word is one and the same, *novyi*).

Certain minor precedents for the civil architecture of St. Petersburg could be found in Russia, to be sure, notably the churches and mansions built in and around Moscow in Peter's early years, or even before his time, in a hybrid "Moscow Baroque" style. The name, invented in the early twentieth century by Russian art scholars, is really a misnomer, as there was little that was truly Baroque about these structures in the accepted European sense of the term. In fact, only some elements of their external and internal decoration might so qualify (Fig. 18). On the other hand, all these structures were commissioned by members of the topmost Muscovite elite, including relatives of Peter's mother, who thereby demonstrated their budding taste for the new architecture emanating from western Europe by way of Poland, the Ukraine, and Belorussia. At the same time, the structures themselves reveal their builders' inability as yet to construct an edifice fully in the Baroque style, itself an outgrowth via Mannerism of Italian Renaissance architecture and a style that by the end of the seventeenth century dominated building in Europe. Nevertheless these structures, some of which survive in Moscow today (Fig. 18), can be considered harbingers of what was to come in Russia, whetting appetites for the real thing.

The question of exactly when and where the seeds of the Petrine revolution in Russian architecture were sown, and of exactly what stylistic form their first blossoms took (Mannerist? Baroque? something else?), need not concern us here. There can be no doubt that European architecture in the Renaissance tradition was finally and fully implanted in Russia only under Peter, and with the help of thousands of imported European builders who worked first at Azov and Voronezh as well as in and around Moscow (we know of only thirty such builders working in Russia during the entire previous century, almost all in fortification). Nor can there be any doubt that this great effort culminated in the construction of St. Petersburg, which for nearly two centuries thereafter remained the center of European architecture in Russia. By 1725, when Peter died, most of the new capital's 40,000 inhabitants still lived, it is true, in dwellings constructed of wood or, at best, wattle-and-daub. But at least the latter, often built after designs by resident European architects, imitated the appearance of contemporary European urban housing. Still more, the city's numerous official or public buildings, designed by the same or other architects, were mostly constructed of brick or stone, and won the respect if not the admiration of every European visitor of the time who has left any record. Most important, in its overall layout as well as its appearance St. Petersburg stood in stark contrast to contemporary Moscow—or any other Russian town. This was a matter of St. Petersburg's free extension, unconfined by city walls; of its straight streets and broad boulevards, versus Moscow's mostly crooked little lanes; and of its regular rows of houses built facing the street rather than any which way, back in the lot, obscured by lean-tos and sheds. Architecturally St. Petersburg was a "modern" city in contemporary European terms, Moscow as yet a "medieval" one.

In the eyes of seventeenth-century European visitors, Moscow's main churches, their cupolas covered in gold leaf, gave the city a superficially splendid appearance, as did its fortified walls and grandee mansions (Fig. 19). But such initial impressions, they invariably reported, were deceptive. In the memorable words of Adam Olearius, a German scholar-diplomat who made several trips to Russia, the city "shines like Jerusalem from without but is like Bethlehem within" (Fig. 20).[7] For all its great size (perhaps 200,000 inhabitants), reports another such visitor, its countless churches and bustling markets, Moscow was "on the whole a mess, built without any architectural order or art."[8] Captain John Perry, the naval engineer hired by Peter in England in 1697, describes how Moscow looked in 1698:

> Whenever any traveller comes within a fair view of the city, the numerous churches, the monasteries, and noblemen and gentlemen's houses, the steeples, cupolas and crosses of the tops of the churches, which are gilded and painted over, makes the city look to be one of the most rich and beautiful in the world, as indeed it appeared to me at first sight coming from the Novgorod road, which is the best view of it; but upon a nearer view, you find yourself deceived and disappointed in your expectation. When you come into the streets, the houses, excepting those of the boyars and some few rich men, are everywhere built of wood, after a very mean fashion. The walls or fences between the streets and the houses are made of wood, and the very streets, instead of being paved with stone, are lined or laid with wood.[9]

The view was even less impressive when these same visitors traveled in the Russian provinces, where they found a few traditionally designed masonry churches and noble or merchant houses scattered among a haphazard collection of simple wooden structures liable at any moment to catch fire (the perennial curse of the old Russian town). Such settlements were intersected irregularly by streets surfaced in wood—when surfaced at all—and surrounded by equally crude defense works. The reports of seventeenth-century European visitors to Russia are remarkably convergent in conveying a picture of typically medieval if not primitive townscapes: an urban world that was, to them, scarcely European at all.

Why do we care what these visitors thought? We do so because an influential core of the Russian ruling elite, including the young Tsar Peter himself, came to share their largely negative view of Russia's architectural heritage. Several hundred members of this core elite traveled on official business to Poland, Austria, Italy, Germany, France, Holland, and England in the 1680s and 1690s, as did Peter himself, on his Grand Embassy of 1697–1698. They lived for weeks or months at a time in Warsaw, Vienna, Rome, Leipzig, Dresden, Paris, Amsterdam, London, and other European cities and everywhere experienced the new architecture at first hand. They brought back prints of favorite buildings, illustrated histories and geographies, and architectural books. A taste for the "new" or "modern style," as they began to call it, was thus solidified among the Muscovite elite, a taste that local builders, trained in traditional Muscovite techniques, could not satisfy. The result at first was the hybrid "Moscow Baroque" structures referred to above. But once young Peter was securely in power, nothing could stand in the way.

Dozens and then hundreds of European builders were recruited by Peter's agents to practice in Russia—it is estimated that in his time more than a thousand such masters worked on the construction of St. Petersburg alone—and to teach their skills to their Russian assistants. Architectural schools were established, at first informally and then in more organized fashion, a development that culminated in the founding (1757) of the St. Petersburg Academy of Fine Arts, which quickly became a European-class institution for the training of architects as well as painters, sculptors, and graphic artists. Textbooks had to be prepared for the Russian students, the most notable of which was an illustrated Russian translation of Vignola's *The Rule of the Five Orders of Architecture* first published in Rome in 1562. This book was probably the most popular architectural manual in early modern Europe, where it went through countless editions and translations. Russian editions of the Vignola were published in Moscow in 1709, 1712, 1722, and frequently thereafter, making it the single best-known work on architecture in eighteenth-century Russia.

The European masters recruited by Peter and then by his immediate successors trained dozens of Russian students in the new architecture and related interior decoration, and they in turn trained hundreds more of their Russian apprentices. All worked on commissions for the ruler and his or her relatives, for other members of the ruling elite, and for more ordinary nobles and officials eager to emulate their superiors. Numerous palaces and government buildings were thus constructed in variants of the new style, but so too were innumerable noble townhouses and country seats, at first in and around St. Petersburg, then in and around Moscow and beyond. Newly built churches preserved more of the traditional architecture, naturally, for Peter's church reform did not extend to dogma or ritual. But even here incursions of the new style were obvious and at times dominant, especially in churches built in St. Petersburg and on the suburban estates of the rulers and leading grandees. New towns were laid out in Russia in accordance with the new principles of "regular" town planning first fully implemented in St. Petersburg; and old towns or buildings, devastated by fire or grown decrepit with age, were built or rebuilt "regularly [*reguliarno*], as in St. Petersburg," as Peter decreed in May 1723. Thus were the techniques, norms, and values of the new architecture diffused in Russia from his time on, with St. Petersburg as the center of spread. They even reached into the peasant villages of the vast Russian hinterland, forever altering their traditional architectural forms and haphazard layouts. In August 1722 Peter decreed that to control the spread of fire and "for the sake of better construction" villages were to be built or rebuilt (after a fire) in accordance with a new "plan": houses and yards were to be standard in size and to maintain a set distance between them, and the houses themselves were to face forward, in a straight line, flush with a would-be street. Under Catherine II, Peter's self-conscious imitator in this as in so many other respects, the St. Petersburg government directed the planning or renovation of more than 400 cities and towns, all to give the Russian built environment, as Catherine put it, a "more European appearance."[10]

In sum, the Petrine revolution in Russian architecture affected every aspect of the building art and sooner or later reached into every part of the Russian Empire, working transformations in the built environment unimaginable in an earlier age. Initially a matter of necessity with respect to fortification and shipbuilding but essentially one of taste with regard to civil architecture, the revolution can be viewed as a process whereby the principles of contemporary European architecture were deliberately brought to Russia, there to be so firmly implanted in the first decades of the eighteenth century that they determined the subsequent course of Russian architectural history. Much the same may be said for the fate of the other visual arts under Peter and his immediate successors, particularly painting, sculpture, and the graphic arts of drawing, etching, and engraving. Before Peter's time these arts were practiced in Russia, when they were practiced at all, in a typically medieval or, but rarely, very tentatively modern fashion. Our standard of comparison is once again contemporary European art in the Renaissance tradition, which embraced the "new" or "modern" forms of imagery and the allied techniques of image-making that Peter was to propagate in Russia in preference to the visual art of his Muscovite heritage. We turn now to this second main aspect of the Petrine cultural revolution.

The term "Renaissance" is commonly applied to visual art produced in Italy in the fifteenth and sixteenth centuries that manifests a deliberate imitation of ancient Greek or Roman patterns or a conscious return to Classical norms. The word "renaissance" itself, from Italian *rinascita,* or "rebirth," was coined at the time by self-styled "humanist" scholars to mark their cultivation of elements of ancient learning and visual art that had been lost, neglected, or debased during the Middle Ages and their consequent revival of Classical or "humane" culture. This revival happened first in Italy itself and then, following Italian models, in France, Spain, Germany, England, and elsewhere in Europe. From newly discovered or newly reassessed ancient writings and from surviving or newfound relics of Classical art, Renaissance scholars and artists and their patrons learned to value naturalism in imagery and to seek the actuality in sculpture, the illusion in painting, of three-dimensional reality. The result was a revolutionary new style of representation compared with that of the medieval artist, who was concerned not with imitating nature but only with arranging conventional figures and symbols in certain predetermined ways so as to tell a religious story.

Among the achievements of Renaissance art were an entirely unprecedented mastery of perspective and anatomy, a wholly new emphasis on drawing or "design" both as an art in itself and as a preparation for painting, and an equally new command of color and light and shade, the last greatly facilitated by the introduction of oil-based paints in place of egg tempera and of canvas instead of wooden supports. The Renaissance in Italy witnessed the revival of the fresco, or painting on wet plaster walls; the rebirth of the medalist's art; the introduction of the framed, self-contained easel painting; the proliferation of naturalistic sculpture in marble, bronze, lead, wax, plaster, alabaster, or clay; and the debut of the engraved or etched print. Naturalistic portraiture became highly fashionable, the landscape came into its own, and Classical history and mythology were accepted as sources of imagery alongside the Bible and Christian teachings. The growth of secular portraiture and the resort to Classical themes, together with the pursuit of naturalism in style, suggest that for all its still overtly religious content, a secular imperative was implicit in Renaissance imagery from the outset. At any rate, portraits and statues of secular figures, local landscapes and urban scenes, depictions of battles on land and sea, and so-called genre pictures of everyday life assumed increasing prominence as Renaissance art left its Italian homeland and evolved through a "Mannerist" phase to become dominant in "Baroque" forms all over Europe by the end of the seventeenth century. But scarcely any of this amazing fluorescence of new visual art had as yet reached Russia.

Baroque artists sought to assert or reassert Renaissance visual values—naturalism, correct design, harmonious composition, reverence for antiquity, and so forth—while creating magnificent displays intended to celebrate dynasty, church, and aristocracy. The Baroque visual arts, far more than those of the Renaissance proper, were arts of power designed to glorify society's rulers and to magnify their claims, a point that was not lost on Tsar Peter when traveling in Europe in 1697–1698 and again in 1716–1717. The new art and architecture were implanted by him in Russia mainly in Baroque forms. But he was personally attracted to pictures of the more modest Dutch school, whose artists had achieved an unrivaled mastery of realism. In fact, Peter's collection of Dutch marine paintings, portraits, landscapes, still lifes, and genre scenes bought in Amsterdam and hung in his favorite small palace—called Monplaisir—at Peterhof, constituted the first art gallery ever established in Russia. His example in this respect was promptly followed by leading members of his company, including Prince Menshikov, Field Marshal Bruce, and Count Matveev, and then by every noble house in Russia worthy of the name.

Peter's whole-hearted conversion to the norms of the new visual art, followed by a comparable conversion of most of the ruling elite, obviously marked the turning point in this aspect of his cultural revolution. But European influences in Muscovite imagery, paralleling those in Muscovite architecture, had been preparing the ground for decades. A growing taste for naturalistic portraiture at the Muscovite court, for example, had produced pictures of rulers or grandees that exhibited some features of the new art. They were painted by foreign or local masters working in considerable isolation from the European mainstream, however, as the surviving examples of their work, more often effigies than true portraits, plainly attest (Figs. 3, 11). The sacred imagery of Muscovy, the ubiquitous holy icons painted in tempera on church walls or wood panels in the timeworn Byzantine tradition, similarly showed signs of the new visual art—more naturalistic facial features here, more realistic details of dress or setting there, sporadic attempts at linear perspective, and sharper drawing at times (Fig. 21). Yet these traces of the new art certainly did not signal the advent of a Russian renaissance. Moreover, the main source of the new imagery entering Russia in these years was engravings or etchings printed in Holland or Germany, whose exquisite designs and naturalistic depictions of scenes from the Bible understandably dazzled their Russian beholders, encouraging more or less inept imitations. To take just one well-documented case: an engraving depicting a moment in the life of St. Philip as recounted in the Acts of the Apostles and found in an illustrated bible first published at Amsterdam in 1650, an engraving that reproduced a drawing by the noted Dutch artist Maerten van Heemskerck (1498–1574), inspired four different murals painted in Russia in the last years of the seventeenth century as well as two separately painted panel icons.[11] Here now were Russian patrons and artists reaching as best they could for that greater naturalism and finer design in imagery that had long been attracting their counterparts all over Europe, where the revolutionary new medium of print had also served as the initial and in some cases the main agency diffusing Renaissance art.

The decisive event in Peter's conversion to the norms of the new art and in that of his immediate entourage was their Grand Embassy to Europe of 1697–1698. Then and there, in north Germany, Holland, England, and Austria, they viewed the new imagery along with the new architecture in all its Renaissance, Mannerist, and Baroque glory. They visited churches and palaces, bought paintings and engravings, hired at least five artists for service in Russia, and sat for their likenesses to be painted or drawn. Peter's portrait was painted among others by the most famous portraitist of the time in London, the German-born, Dutch- and Italian-trained Sir Godfrey (Gottfried) Kneller. The portrait presents a full-length figure in oil, the pose, dress, and setting quite artificial following Kneller's customary courtly style. But the telescope Peter is shown gripping and the warship looming in the background obviously symbolize the soaring naval ambitions that had brought him to England (Fig. 22). Contemporaries considered the face a remarkably good likeness, ensuring that engraved copies were widely distributed. Peter himself was so taken with the portrait that he ordered a large quantity of miniatures painted after its head and shoulders by a well-known local artist, Charles Boit. These miniatures he then handed out, following the European fashion, to the monarchs, princes, and other high-ranking persons he met on his diplomatic rounds and later, once home, to those of his subjects whose services especially pleased him. Kneller's portrait in one form or another became the first official portrait of a Russian ruler. Equally, one of the Boit miniatures soon became a model for Russian artists working in Moscow. Passable copies were produced in the royal workshops, enabling the tsar to continue his practice of bestowing them on deserving officials and friends (Fig. 23). Similar miniatures were painted of Prince Menshikov (Fig. 1), Tsarevich Aleksei, and other grandees. Thus was born the Russian fashion, eventually a passion among the elite, of giving miniature portraits painted in oil on enamel as keepsakes or mementos of loved ones or as treasured marks of the monarch's favor. In all these Petrine portraits and miniatures, we might also note, the sitter is depicted in contemporary European, not traditional Russian, dress.

In Amsterdam in 1698 Peter himself took lessons in etching.

His teacher was Adriaan Schoonebeck, a leading etcher and publisher of prints who went on to execute numerous commissions for the tsar—etchings of warships (Fig. 9), fireworks, military victories (Figs. 8, 10), maps, portraits, and architectural views—and to set up the first print shop in Russia. There he trained, among others, the first Russian graphic artist of any real standing, Aleksei Zubov. Zubov opened his own print shop in Moscow in 1710; his numerous commissions from Peter (Fig. 4) include early views of Peterhof (Fig. 24) and of St. Petersburg (Fig. 33), precious documents in the history both of the city and of graphic art in Russia. Peter's only known etching, executed in Amsterdam in 1698 under Schoonebeck's supervision, was based on a medal that was cast in Holland in 1696 to commemorate his victory over the Turks at Azov and depicted the event in fairly typical Baroque symbolic forms (Fig. 25).[12] His pride in the victory is thereby affirmed but so too is the strength of his commitment to the new imagery.

Meanwhile, the parallel conversion of leading members of the Muscovite elite is plain to see, for example, in the detailed diary of Peter (later Count) Tolstoy, who had been sent by the tsar to Venice in 1697–1699 to study navigation and related subjects. Tolstoy's reactions to Rome, as recorded there, were little short of euphoric: Rome with its "two thousand churches and monasteries and all most splendidly built, with astonishing ornamentation inside and gloriously decorated outside with wondrously carved magnificent alabaster and marble floral ornaments"; Rome with its fountains "equipped with such magnificent figures that for their multitude nobody could truly describe them"; Rome with its basilica of St. Peter, the "largest church in the world and most marvelously constructed," its "canopy and columns carved in the most marvelous fashion," its "wonderfully carved angels, all splendidly gilded," its interior "all magnificently done in white marble, with the most wonderful alabaster carving," its "paintings on the walls and ceilings in the most magnificent, glorious Italian style."[13] Similar impressions were recorded in the diaries, notebooks, or diplomatic correspondence of other Russians traveling west at this time, Russians like Count Matveev (Fig. 14), whose knowledge of contemporary European art and particularly of the French art world gained from his residence in Paris (1705–1706) would be influential not only in the spread of the new taste in Russia but in the eventual foundation of the St. Petersburg Academy of Fine Arts.[14]

Peter's revolution in Russian imagery largely followed the course of his concurrent architectural revolution, not surprisingly, as the two were at many points closely interrelated. Dutch, German, French, and Italian artists were recruited to work and teach in Russia, and sizable collections of paintings, prints, and sculptures executed in the European Renaissance tradition were assembled in the Moscow, St. Petersburg, and suburban or country residences of the monarch and leading grandees, their example soon followed by lesser nobles and their kin. Print shops and studios were set up; Russian art students were sent to the Netherlands, France, or Italy to complete their training; and the collections of Peter and his immediate successors were converted into the first public art galleries in Russia, accessible for viewing and study by art students and the elite public. Within half a century of Peter's death St. Petersburg could boast of one of the largest assemblages of such art in Europe and of an art academy of European-class distinction. From its founding in 1757 by Empress Elizabeth, Peter's daughter, the St. Petersburg Academy of Fine Arts was the center of an enormous expansion of the new art in Russia, having produced within fifty years more than 700 painters, sculptors, architects, and graphic artists whose work was disseminated from one end of the Empire to the other. In the words of one Russian art historian, the Academy "directed the entire artistic life of the country in the eighteenth and first half of the nineteenth centuries."[15] In this respect, as in architecture, Russia had entered the European mainstream.

Nor was the Petrine revolution in Russian imagery restricted to fine or elite art. The cult art of the Russian Orthodox church was more or less directly affected too, though again, as in church architecture, less so than other forms of imagery. After Peter the church retained its religious traditions intact, only its governance had been changed and its educational standards raised. A somewhat analogous development took place in popular or folk art. Over the centuries after Peter, until it largely expired in Soviet times, Russian folk art produced a fascinating fusion of traditional peasant forms (suns, flowers, birds, animals, mermaids) and new-art or high-art elements whether in ornament, in new genre scenes (tea drinking, promenading, riding in carriages or sleighs), or in details of dress, gesture, and background.[16]

More important, perhaps, was the revolution's effect on what might be called official imagery, or the visual representations of their status and power projected by Peter and his successors for the purpose of enhancing their prestige in Europe and reinforcing their rule at home. Such imagery included, in addition to the innumerable painted or engraved portraits already mentioned, symbolic representations of themselves and their state produced on seals and medals and properly minted coins, on flags and banners, on the insignia of the new knightly orders and in the new noble heraldry, and in porcelain (the famous dinner sets manufactured by the Imperial china factories) and tapestry (produced, again, by an Imperial factory established under Peter with the help of Gobelins in France). With the exception of coins, the official-noble elite were the prime consumers or beneficiaries of this new imagery, of course, which in turn helped unify them into a distinctive ruling class with a vision of itself as the cultural, social, and political core of the Russian Empire. It was this elite who proudly wore the new coats-of-arms and medals and knightly orders handed out by the monarch, who served as officers in the army and navy under the new flags and banners, who ate off the Imperial plates and admired the Imperial tapestries, and who flaunted their officer commissions and diplomas of nobility emblazoned with the new state seal. Coins, by contrast, were for anybody who could get their hands on them, and under Peter a regular decimalized monetary system, embodied in an up-to-date coinage minted in unprecedented quantities in gold, silver, and copper, was introduced in Russia. The new coins all bore newly devised or newly redesigned symbols of the monarch and the Empire complete with embossed dates and mintmarks, all as done in the best European monetary systems. Between 1701 and 1724 anywhere from half a million to 4.5 million rubles' worth of the new silver coins were minted annually (much smaller quantities in copper and gold), or something like five to ten times the annual mint totals of pre-Petrine times. And along with the coins thus being dispersed to the far corners of Russia went the new political images, with the tsar in the guise now of a Roman emperor, a symbolic visage very like that of the contemporary Austrian emperor on his coins or those of the kings of England and France on theirs (Fig. 26).

Nor was that all. Under Peter Russia was properly mapped for the first time, with very considerable political and even psychological implications. Maps shape human conceptions of space beyond what is immediately visible; hence they have always had valence as means of codifying and legitimizing as well as actually effecting territorial expansion and control. In Europe since the Renaissance maps not only presented geographical information in ever more accurate visual form but, with their lines indicating longitude and latitude, their networks of political jurisdictions, their regal portraits and captions, and their images of conquered peoples, mythological figures, and important towns, they conveyed ideas of their owners' knowledge and power. Such maps were valued, collected, and displayed accordingly. But no such maps existed in Russia before Peter's time, and Europeans included "Muscovy" on their maps of Europe only as a vague eastern borderland. In fact, Russians first acquired the mapmaking skills that had evolved in Europe since about 1500, and the more accurate and comprehensive maps of their country that could be

thereby produced, in connection with Peter's administrative reforms. It was yet another way for Peter to establish his state as a
European power and to govern it more effectively.

Once again the steps followed those of the Petrine cultural revolution more generally. Experts were imported from Europe, Russian surveyors and cartographers were trained, detailed surveys of
the country were conducted using the latest astronomical methods, maps were engraved and printed, and an appropriate office—
the Geography Department of the St. Petersburg Academy of
Sciences—was organized, all at great expense. By 1765 the Academy had produced some 300 maps of many previously uncharted
or vaguely charted areas of Russia and the world. By far the most
important of these productions was the general atlas of the Russian Empire (*Atlas Russica*) first published by the Academy's press
in 1745 in Latin, French, German, and two Russian editions. With
this atlas, which had been in preparation for more than twenty
years, Russia was at once mapped more or less in accordance with
the best European standards and "put on the map," in both Russian and European eyes. The vastness of the Empire was now plain
for all to see, as were, at last, its northern, eastern, and southern
borders. The continental line between Europe and Asia was drawn
at the Ural mountains, with the Russian Empire clearly divided
into a European heartland and colonial or semi-colonial Asian
provinces. It was a stunning cartographical achievement, and
more: a critical question of Russian identity, and of Europe's as a
whole, was visually resolved. After 1745 maps of Europe published
anywhere in Europe depicted Russia—"European Russia"—as an
integral part of Europe, and the Urals as Europe's boundary with
Asia. And so, geographically, they have remained.

The core of any human culture worthy of the name is not
visual, however, but verbal. This brings us to the third main aspect
of Peter's cultural revolution to be considered here, for drastic
changes in language occurred in Russia in his time, too. Mapping
Russia, for example, entailed the hiring of French astronomers

and cartographers and the learning, by their Russian students, of all the new technical terms involved. Creating a navy, to take a bigger and still more obvious case, required the recruitment of Dutch, Italian, and British shipwrights and officers to teach the appropriate skills to Russians; the translation into Russian of Dutch, Italian, and English manuals on navigation and ship-building; and the adoption by Russians of the related technical vocabularies—hence another, much bigger increase in the Russian lexicon. But it went further than that. To expedite the translation of all the European technical manuals and legal, historical, scientific, and other works required to implement Peter's various projects, Russian spelling, syntax, and punctuation had to be standardized in keeping with contemporary European norms. A new system of numbering (the standard European one) also had to be adopted and a new alphabet devised, one that would be more suitable for printing all the new texts than were the cumbersome letters of traditional Cyrillic. In fact, the European print revolution, which as much as anything else had marked the transition from the medieval to the modern era in Europe itself, had to be brought at last to Russia. This Peter also did.[17]

The new craft of printing, which entailed the mechanical production of printed sheets by means of screw-press and movable metal types, a feat first achieved in certain German towns in the middle of the fifteenth century, arrived in Muscovy only in the 1550s. Over the next decade or two some sixteen titles were printed, all religious in content—a tiny fraction of the thousands of religious but also literary, philosophical, scientific, and technical titles and editions printed *annually* in the several hundred print shops established all over Europe by this time. This initial effort to found both printing presses and the necessary paper mills in Muscovy soon collapsed for lack of adequate official support, enough literate consumers, even among the clergy, and widespread hostility to what was perceived as the devilish invention of foreigners. Printing revived in Russia only in the 1620s, after the

Time of Troubles, and between then and the 1690s fewer than 500 titles were issued, nearly all of them devotional books and nearly all produced at a single shop controlled by the Moscow patriarch. The few non-religious titles included the *Ulozhenie* or law code of 1649 and a grammar of Church Slavonic, the archaic, highly stylized language of the Orthodox churches of Russia, Ukraine, Belorussia, Serbia, and Bulgaria. Moreover, throughout the seventeenth century Russians still had to import all their paper for printing from abroad, an expensive proposition given the distances such paper had to travel—typically, from France overland and by sea to Archangel, and from there by river and road down to Moscow.

Paper mills were permanently established in Russia under Peter, and mainly in response to the huge increase in printing that occurred during his reign. By 1719 the consumption of paper in Russia had risen from the 4,000 to 8,000 reams imported annually in the late seventeenth century to some 50,000 reams a year, of which only about 10 percent were imported; the rest were produced by the five mills founded in Russia between 1708 and 1718 with the help of Dutch, German, and Swedish craftsmen. At the same time, Peter started new print shops, or *tipografii,* as he called them, borrowing the common European word (typography). By the end of his reign four shops were functioning in St. Petersburg in addition to the old Printing House in Moscow (another would soon open, at the St. Petersburg Academy of Sciences, in 1726). Their combined output, meaning the total number of books, booklets, pamphlets, and single sheets printed in Russia between 1700 and Peter's death in January 1725, in press-runs of anywhere from a few dozen to a few thousand or more copies (the average edition was 300 to 600), has been put at 1,312. Of these, 308 titles were religious in content, the rest, secular, a number that includes the many technical and other works needed to implement Peter's various reform projects or to enlighten his elite as well as his numerous charters, regulations, and decrees.[18] This twenty-five-year total of more than 1,300 titles is considerably more than twice the number, almost all of them religious, published during the entire previous century and a half of printing in Russia.

To facilitate this huge burst of printing an alphabet reform was required. The existing Cyrillic alphabet had originated in the medieval Slavic lands to transcribe the language that came to be known as Church Slavonic. It consisted of some forty-odd letters, over half of which were Greek or Greek-based, the rest invented to accommodate Slavic sounds. The careful, clear, uncial (all capitals) style in which these letters were originally written gradually gave way to a less formal, semi-uncial (or semi-cursive) script that was written with frequent ligatures, diacritics, and stress marks along with various abbreviations and contractions. These changes were introduced by busy scribes to make it easier and quicker for them to copy the religious texts needed for the steadily expanding churches of Muscovy and the other Slavic Orthodox lands. The fonts employed by the first printers in those countries naturally were based on this rather esoteric, semi-uncial script, which continued to acquire new letters borrowed from Greek or new letter-shapes borrowed from the Roman and italic styles that had become standard in printing in Europe. Printers in Moscow were much slower to introduce these innovations than were their counterparts in Ukraine and Belorussia; but when it came to the law code of 1649 and the few other secular titles printed in Russia before Peter, a shifting mix of the churchly semi-uncial style and a simpler cursive used by clerks in the tsar's offices, the so-called chancery script, was employed. These diverse practices resulted, as can be readily imagined, in a cumbersome, unstable concatenation of more or less elaborate letters and styles and a correspondingly motley stock of typefaces, a situation that made it difficult to print the increasing number of government documents and technical manuals required by Peter's projects with the speed and efficiency that were now standard all over Europe. Primers published in Moscow in Peter's youth display alphabets of forty-one or forty-five or even forty-seven letters, each printed in a dozen or more variously elaborate shapes.

Peter and his assistants resolved this vexing situation by devising in stages a new alphabet for use in printing all government documents and works of secular content, leaving the traditional Cyrillic alphabet as the basis for printing all "church books." The task was first entrusted to a printer in Amsterdam, Jan Tessing. According to Peter's charter of February 1700, Tessing was to print "for sale throughout our Russian realm" an unspecified number of "European, Asiatic and American land and marine pictures and charts, and all kinds of printed sheets and portraits, and mathematical, architectural, town-planning, military, marine and other art books in the Slavonic and Latin languages together, or in Slavonic and Dutch together or separately, whence the subjects of our royal majesty [Peter] shall receive much use and profit and be instructed in all the arts and specialties, and glory [shall accrue] to our royal majesty's name and to our entire Russian realm among the European monarchs." The privilege was not to extend to the printing of "church Slavonic books of the Greek rite, because church Slavonic Greek books, with the approval of the whole Orthodox authority of the Eastern church, are [already] printed in our royal city of Moscow."[19]

So the fateful division began. Books produced for the Russian market over the next few years by Tessing in Amsterdam included manuals on arithmetic, astronomy, military tactics, navigation, and European or world history; an edition of Aesop's fables and a panegyric celebrating Peter's victory at Azov in 1696; a Latin grammar and a Latin-Russian glossary in verse; two simple lexicons, the first in Russian (not Slavonic), Latin, and German, the second in Russian, Latin, and Dutch; an almanac, a textbook on rhetoric, and a *Manual of Slavonic-Russian or Muscovite Grammar*: more secular titles than had been published in the entire previous history of book printing in Muscovy, Ukraine, and Belorussia put together. Most of this publication had little impact on developments in Russia, however, as the books were written in an alien "Russian" concocted by their Belorussian translator, few copies had been printed, and fewer still reached their intended destination. Yet the fonts designed by Tessing to print his non-church books for the Russian market reflected in varying degrees contemporary European types, a feature of his output that caught the approving eye, as events would show, of Peter and company.

Nor had Peter been content to wait for urgently needed books to be printed in Amsterdam and shipped to Russia via a lengthy and, with the onset of war with Sweden (October 1700), perilous voyage. In 1699 a *Short Standard Instruction for the Organization of Foot Regiments* was printed at the Moscow press and reprinted in 1700 (twice), 1702, and 1704. In 1703 an *Arifmetika* (mathematics textbook) was also printed there, yet another first for Russia. Both books were printed in traditional Cyrillic fonts, to be sure, since nothing else was as yet available. But the texts of both were larded with technical neologisms, not surprisingly given their subjects, and were written in a comparatively "plain" Russian, as Peter had ordered, rather than a highbrow Church Slavonic. Peter was concerned that these books should be readable not just by clerics and divinity students but by the soldiers and would-be soldiers, government clerks and apprentice seamen for whom they were intended. Linguistic as well as typographical traditions were thus being seriously challenged. Later in 1703 a manual of logarithmic tables adapted from a Latin original published at Amsterdam was first printed in Moscow for the use of students at the new Moscow School of Mathematics and Navigation run by a Scotsman, Henry Farquharson, who had been hired by Peter in England in 1698. Here the traditional Slavonic numbering system (using successive letters of the Cyrillic alphabet as numerals) had to be abandoned in favor of the now common European (Arabic) system, something that was also done in the exercises printed in the *Arifmetika*.

In addition, Roman or italic types had to be introduced in both books to print the Latin terms used along with Greek type for the Greek words.

The first issues of the new official *Gazette (Vedomosti)* also appeared in Moscow in 1703. These were printed versions of the manuscript bulletins *(kuranty)* of military and political news from Europe that had long been prepared from foreign, primarily German, sources by clerks, themselves often foreigners, of the Ambassadorial Office in Moscow for circulation within the tsar's government. Now such news, expanded to include domestic Russian, mainly court, developments, was being made available to a considerably wider readership via the new *Gazette,* which therefore is often dubbed Russia's first printed newspaper. The *Gazette* initially appeared in the traditional Cyrillic type, too. But starting with the issue of February 1, 1710, its issues were printed, like successive editions of the logarithmic manual just mentioned, in a new "civil" type, or fonts based on an alphabet that Russian and Dutch craftsmen, following Tessing's example, had invented for printing books and other works of purely secular content. The division between the one and the other, between "church books" printed in the traditional Cyrillic type and secular texts printed in a different, simpler, more European or modern type, was solidifying.

Indeed, as early as 1703 or so Peter had realized that to advance the ambitious publishing program necessitated by his aggressive military, naval, and related educational projects he would have to establish a new alphabetic norm for printing in Russia. The story of how he did so—of how he invented the modern Russian alphabet—has long fascinated scholars. The crucial years were 1708–1710. Reviewing specimens of proposed new types sent to him, ever away on campaign, by the designated Russian and Dutch printers, Peter progressively refined the search until nine letters of the traditional Cyrillic alphabet had been dropped and the rest more or less drastically simplified on the basis of contemporary European types and everyday Moscow chancery script.

This alone would count as a major achievement of the Petrine revolution in Russian culture.

After 1710, again by Peter's decree, issued evidently in deference to the views of the higher clergy, traditional Cyrillic fonts complete with Slavonic numerals were retained in all their ornateness for the printing of all "church books" (Fig. 27). But all secular texts—books, official documents, academic journals, and so on—were to be printed in appropriately streamlined "civil" fonts (Fig. 28). The traditional Cyrillic alphabet and corresponding typefaces became in effect the property of the Orthodox church, where they had, indeed, originated. At the same time, the civil alphabet and related typefaces, elicited in stages from the traditional Cyrillic under the influence of Latin and Moscow chancery norms, became with only minor changes thereafter the standard for all other printing—in short, the modern Russian norm. It is true that more copies of church books, particularly catechisms and service manuals, continued to be printed and distributed in Russia after 1710. But in the volume and variety of titles published in the new civil rather than the traditional Cyrillic type, there was no contest. Inventories of eighteenth-century Russian book publication indicate that while some 1,500 titles were printed in Cyrillic, the total number printed in civil types from 1710 on was about 10,000, a nearly seven-to-one preponderance.

Nor did Peter confine his linguistic reform to devising a new alphabet. He insisted from early on that the new technical handbooks, scientific treatises, etiquette manuals, history books, and other works to be translated from Latin, German, Dutch, or Italian originals, and any government regulations or other such texts to be composed anew, should all be written in a "plain" or "simple" (*prostoi*) style. By this he meant a language readily accessible not just to the learned clerical elite of the day, adept at Church Slavonic, but to the intended readership of military and naval personnel, diplomats, technocrats, and bureaucrats, natural scientists and other purely secular scholars, artists, architects, and skilled craftsmen, and students training to pursue these employments. It was a language purged of the more recondite Slavonic grammatical forms, stock words and phrases, and esoteric scribal devices, and written in a more straightforward Russian vernacular style. The new language was replete with new loan words and strove to emulate, as occasion required and the writer's skill permitted, contemporary European literary norms. The Petrine plain style, in short, formed the basis of the modern Russian literary language, which was gradually "stabilized," as linguists say, over the course of the eighteenth century with the publication of Russian grammar books and dictionaries and the creation of a Russian literary canon—activities that also began under Peter. Meanwhile Church Slavonic, its rich old word stock regularly mined by Russian linguists in search of Slavic roots, was soon frozen in its traditional role as the formal language of the official church and some of its sectarian offshoots. And so it has remained.

But the linguistic impact of the Petrine revolution was most obvious in the realm of lexicon, with the introduction of an enormous number of new words. Scholars have identified some 4,500 individual loan words that entered Russian in the Petrine period (ca. 1695–1725), as compared with about 760 in the preceding thirty or so years: more than a six-fold increase. (It might be noted that only about 1,000 new words entered English in the two centuries between 1500 and 1700, as did a roughly similar total between 1700 and 1900, indicating both that English had a richer lexicon by about 1500 than did Russian and that lexical enhancement was a more gradual process in English.) The basic sources of this enormous influx were of course the numerous translations undertaken in Peter's time from German, Dutch, Italian, Latin, French, English, and Swedish originals. More often than not, it is also worth noting, the Russian translators simply russified the many new technical, legal, and other words encountered in the originals rather than try to invent Russian equivalents (calques).

Scholars have found many such neologisms in the surviving correspondence of Peter and members of the elite, in Petrine legislation, and in original works written in Russian at the time (such as Shafirov's *Discourse* of 1717) as well as in the numerous translations done on Peter's orders. To be sure, many of the new words more or less rapidly became obsolete: the several hundred nautical terms borrowed from Dutch and English to name the parts of a fully rigged sailing ship and from Italian to designate those of an oar-powered galley are cases in point. So are many of the military terms borrowed mainly from German to designate weapons that were soon outmoded or to name elements of early modern fortification and siegecraft that later became obsolete. Numerous Germanic political and administrative terms borrowed by Peter's regime in reforming the state—names for officials and their offices, terms of bureaucratic protocol, and so on—were also sooner or later outmoded, or simply remained foreign in Russian. Even so, the number of new words that were fixed in Russian during the thirty or so years of Peter's active reign and of Russian derivations that were quickly formed from these words (usually adjectives, verbs, or adverbs formed from new nouns) was entirely unprecedented in Russia or, very likely, anywhere else in so short a time. When the semantic range of all these neologisms is considered, the breadth of subjects and meanings involved, this lexical influx alone is nothing short of revolutionary.[20]

More specifically, of the roughly 600 nautical terms that entered Russian in the Petrine era, some half remain in use; and many of these gained new applications, as they did elsewhere, with the advent of airplanes and then of spacecraft. Several hundred military terms were similarly fixed in Russian in Peter's time, remaining in use to this day. In both of these arenas, it may be said, the Petrine verbal influx was foundational: the bases of modern Russian naval and military thought were thus laid, "thought" understood to mean the capacity for precise verbalization, now in

Russian, of all the new tactics, strategies, maneuvers, weapons, and equipment that Peter's regime had brought into play. This was no less true of the new official vocabulary adopted in Russian under Peter, the terminology of political modernization, as we might call it, or the administrative, legal, and diplomatic language of the modern European state. This language was now employed, suitably russified, in implementing Peter's bureaucratic and diplomatic revolutions and in articulating his doctrine of absolute monarchy. Many hundreds of mathematical, medical, musical, literary, art and architectural, philosophical, technological, and scientific terms were borrowed from German, Latin, Dutch, French, English, Italian, and Polish in Peter's time, too, becoming as basic in the modern Russian lexicon as they are in the lexicons of these other languages. Several dozen important commercial or industrial words were similarly borrowed (bank, banker, book-keeper, inventory, factory, mine), as were numerous new words for fine food and drink (artichokes, celery, oysters, coffee, candy, champagne), fancy clothes (necktie, camisole, cuff, dressing gown), entertainments (fireworks, ballet, billiards, social "assemblies" of both men and women), exotic fruits and flowers (figs, apricots, peaches, oranges, tulips), tableware (goblets, napkins, dinner service) and other utensils (umbrella, casserole, fan), furniture (ward-robe), living quarters (apartment, hall), and so on. These are only a few examples of the hundreds, indeed thousands of new words pouring into Russian in Peter's time, words which, to repeat, by themselves denote a wide-ranging cultural revolution of immense historical significance. Russian society was thus being irrevocably brought, if at first mainly at the elite level, into the European mainstream, the sphere of modernity.

The St. Petersburg Academy of Sciences was in many ways the epitome of this verbal revolution—indeed, of the Petrine cultural revolution more generally. Its genesis can be traced to Peter's visit to the Royal Society of London in 1698 and to his subsequent contacts, particularly through James Bruce, with what was then generally considered the most distinguished of the new scientific societies in Europe. The great Isaac Newton (whom Peter may well have met; Bruce certainly did) was the Society's longtime president and it was to Newton, in that capacity, that the St. Petersburg Academy of Sciences addressed its first formal communication, in Latin, on October 11, 1726.[21] But the idea of founding such an institution in Russia certainly had other sources, too, most notably Peter's correspondence from 1697 and several subsequent meetings with another great figure of the Scientific Revolution, Gottfried W. Leibniz, the father of the Berlin Academy of Sciences. Then there was Peter's visit to the Paris Academy of Sciences in 1717, and his ongoing contacts with that venerable institution of royal science. His gradual buildup, from early in his reign, of a scientific library and collection of scientific specimens and instruments and his ever-expanding cartographic projects also pointed to the necessity of creating an academy both to house and administer it all and to plan for the future—not to mention the desirability of establishing parity in this respect with the "other" European monarchs. Equally relevant here were Peter's multifarious activities as "the Father of Russian medicine."[22]

Peter was the first (and only) Russian ruler to learn the rudiments of modern medicine and surgery, to observe medical procedures firsthand, and to frequent medical institutions both at home and abroad. In Holland in 1697–1698 he visited hospitals, botanical gardens, and insane asylums. He also attended medical lectures at the University of Leiden—where Herman Boerhaave was pioneering the new, clinically oriented surgery based on the study of anatomy through dissection of corpses—and visited Dr. Fredrik Ruysch's famous anatomical museum in Amsterdam. On his return visit to Holland in 1717 he bought up Ruysch's anatomical collections and had them shipped to St. Petersburg, where remnants are still on view in the Kunstkamera or "Cabinet of Curiosities" that he founded as Russia's first museum (Fig. 29).

Some fifty surgeons were recruited for the nascent Russian

navy in Holland in 1698, and on Peter's orders a Dutch physician, Dr. Nicolaas Bidloo, was hired to build a hospital and surgical school in Moscow, yet again the first institutions of their kind in Russia. By 1723 Bidloo's school had trained at least 73 Russian medical personnel—some 800 by the end of the eighteenth century—and had facilitated the founding of nine hospitals in St. Petersburg and other Russian towns. Two of the new hospitals were under Admiralty auspices and soon added their own surgical schools, all as provided in the "Hospital Statute" contained in Peter's *Admiralty Regulation* of 1722. This document drew considerably on the French naval ordinance of 1689 and heavily influenced in turn the general regulation of 1735 governing all hospitals in Russia.[23] Meanwhile, army medical services had been regularized in Peter's *Military Statute* of 1716, which provided that surgeons were to be assigned to every regiment and supported by paramedics and portable pharmacies.

The only medical institution that predated Peter's reign in Russia was the Apothecary Office in Moscow, which originated in the sixteenth century. It was staffed by foreign medical specialists assisted, after 1653, by Russians; but it remained an office of the tsar's household, whose members and various dependents, except in time of war, it served almost exclusively.[24] Peter, by contrast, chartered eight private apothecary shops in Moscow designed to serve the public and supported the studies abroad, at the universities of Padua, Paris, and Leiden, of the first certified Russian medical doctor, Peter Postnikov. Moreover, two of his personal physicians, following a pattern that was common in Europe at the time, played critical roles in the founding of his Academy of Sciences.

The first of these physicians was the Scot Robert Erskine, who entered Russian service in 1704, was appointed head of the Apothecary Office in 1707, and in 1713 became *lieb-medik,* or personal physician to the tsar. In this position he also supervised medical education and the hiring of foreign medical personnel, oversaw the founding of the Medical Chancery in St. Petersburg, of which he then became head, and took charge of Peter's burgeoning library and scientific collections, which were moved to the new capital in 1714 and lodged in his newly built Summer Palace. Also in 1714 one Johann Daniel Schumacher arrived from Germany, a graduate with honors of Strassburg University, to become Erskine's assistant with special responsibility for organizing the tsar's library and *kabinet* of scientific "curiosities." In fact, the lodging of Peter's books and scientific collections in the Summer Palace in 1714 under Erskine's supervision and Schumacher's direct control has been taken to mark the founding of the Academy's Library (now a world-class institution) and associated Kunstkamera, or natural history museum (from German *Kunstkammer*), both of which were soon housed in their own building (Fig. 29). Erskine died in 1718 and was succeeded as the tsar's personal physician and senior medical official by Laurentius Blumentrost, who had been born in Moscow in 1692, the son of a German physician in the tsar's service, and had studied under Boerhaave at Leiden. Blumentrost went on to become the first president of the St. Petersburg Academy of Sciences, for whose actual establishment he was largely responsible.

To make a long story short, after seeking advice from colleagues in Germany and sending Schumacher on an extended trip around northern Europe to buy books and scientific instruments and to recruit interested scholars, Blumentrost submitted a detailed *Project* to Peter sometime late in 1723. In it he proposed to found in Russia, "after the example of other states," an "institution for promoting the arts and sciences." It was to be called an academy but would combine the features of a research center and a teaching university (since Russia lacked both), and thereby "not only redound to the glory of this state for increasing the sciences at the present time, but through teaching and disseminating them would benefit the people in future." Peter instantly accepted the proposal, arrangements for its financing were made, and on

January 28, 1724, a decree was issued announcing the Academy's foundation. A special "Academy office" was promptly set up to handle the relevant correspondence, the groundwork was laid in St. Petersburg for a permanent building designed, naturally, in the new style (it would be ready in 1726), and announcements of the Academy's establishment were circulated in Europe along with invitations to join it.

By the end of 1725 sixteen German, Swiss, and French scholars, all highly qualified, some even distinguished, had settled in St. Petersburg and taken up their appointments. They included two astronomers, a zoologist and surgeon, three mathematicians, a Classical scholar, two "natural philosophers" specializing in physics and another in chemistry and medicine, and several "moral philosophers" adept in history, eloquence, and law. Informal meetings of the new Academy were held in St. Petersburg in the summer of 1725, and its first formal gathering took place in November. Peter himself, the Academy's founder and first patron, died on January 28, 1725. But there was no turning back. It became Academy lore that "Peter, falling sick some time after the foundation of the Academy, in his last moments earnestly requested the Empress Catherine, who was to succeed him, to put the finishing hand to the work."[25] Indeed, Catherine soon ratified the *Project* of 1724 and formally nominated Blumentrost to be the Academy's first president. Schumacher was confirmed as its first secretary as well as its first librarian, positions he continued to occupy, consolidating the Academy's administrative structure, assiduously guarding its interests, until his retirement in 1759 (Blumentrost remained president until 1733).[26]

It is common knowledge that the St. Petersburg Academy of Sciences, from its birth a European rather than a narrowly Russian institution, went on to achieve international fame in mathematics, physics, chemistry, psychology, and other fields of scientific endeavor. Less well known is the role it played in disseminating science and the new culture more broadly within Russia itself. Its use of Latin in its formal proceedings and related publications during its first decades, for one thing, introduced Russian students to the language used by the contemporary European learned world, and thereby facilitated the assimilation in Russian of current scientific, academic, and other scholarly concepts and terms. Its press was the single most important shop publishing scientific, literary, and other secular works in Russia until the end of the eighteenth century, just as its staff included, for many years, the ablest translators working in Russia and the compilers of the first grammars and dictionaries of Russian. Its print shop was the most important center of the new graphic arts in Russia until the Academy of Fine Arts was founded in 1757. Various of its first academicians, Germans though they originally were, served in the Academy with distinction for many years and laid the foundations in Russia not only of the natural sciences but of archaeology, geography, and history as well.

Dozens of Russian youths were trained in science and foreign languages in the St. Petersburg Academy's first classes. By 1733, less than a decade after its establishment, one of these students, V. E. Adodurov, had been appointed adjunct (teacher) in mathematics; he was also an accomplished translator from German, taught Russian to the future Empress Catherine II (German by birth), in 1762 was appointed by her administrator of the recently founded Moscow University, and in 1778 was named an honorary academician. Adodurov was followed at the Academy by G. N. Teplov (adjunct in botany, 1742, full academician from 1747), M. V. Lomonosov (adjunct in physics, 1742, professor of chemistry from 1745), V. K. Trediakovsky (professor of eloquence, 1745), and S. T. Krasheninnikov (adjunct in natural history, 1745, professor of botany and natural history from 1750). They in turn were followed, from the 1750s until the end of the eighteenth century, by the appointment of another twenty-four Russians (along with sixty foreigners) to senior positions in the Academy. Among the rising native stars, one, Teplov, went on to write the first philosophy textbook in Russian, while both Lomonosov and Trediakovsky made important contributions to the creation of modern Russian literature and the standardization of the modern Russian literary language. Lomonosov was also a scientist of some renown and a founder of Moscow University.

Still more, it could be said that the second university, after Moscow, to be formally founded in Russia, the University of St. Petersburg (1819), was a direct outgrowth of the St. Petersburg Academy of Sciences founded by Peter in 1724. The Academy thus represented the apex of his many and varied educational initiatives, from the primary and secondary naval and military schools discussed in the preceding chapters to the programs for advanced training in visual art and architecture mentioned above. According to its original plan (the *Project* of 1723), the Academy was even supposed to support a department of theology overseen by the Holy Synod. But this proposal was soon abandoned in favor of the separate theological academy called for by the *Ecclesiastical Regulation* of 1721, an institution that gradually took shape in St. Petersburg under the direction of Feofan Prokopovich. It was the first of the four theological academies that would eventually preside over the network of diocesan and parochial schools inaugurated under Peter.

The single most important function of the St. Petersburg Academy of Sciences, to be sure, was to serve from 1725 as the institutional heart of the onrushing effort to naturalize in Russian the concepts and terms of modern European science. Through its teaching, research, and publication, writes the leading American student of its history, "scientific thought spilled over the Academy's rigid confines" during the later eighteenth century "to wash a vast area of Russian culture." In this considered view,

> The social effect of science in eighteenth-century Russia cannot be overemphasized. It destroyed once and for all the intellectual supremacy of the Church, which fed on outmoded

Scholasticism and sacrosanct superstitions; and it became the rallying point for a frontal attack on ignorance. Science gave strength to the emergent national consciousness of the Russian people; the results of historical and geographical research and of its scientific expeditions were reflected in a broader and more widely distributed literature. As teachers, writing and translating books, the scientists also led the struggle to raise the educational level of the Russian people. Slowly and painstakingly, they made the Russian language a vehicle of scientific communication.[27]

The assessment is a shade positivistic, perhaps, even grandiose. But it is also essentially true, no doubt, and a handsome tribute to the founder of the Academy and all who helped him bring it into being.

1. Portrait of Alexander Menshikov, 1710s. Miniature in oil on enamel in gold frame, artist unknown. Clean-shaven and wearing a wig, Menshikov is depicted not as a traditional Russian boyar (see Fig. 13) but as a contemporary European grandee. (Russian Museum, St. Petersburg)

2. Ivan Nikitin, portrait of Princess Natalia (sister of Peter I), before 1716. Oil on canvas. Nikitin, who has been called the first Russian portraitist, learned the new European style of painting from masters working in Russia and then at art academies in Florence and Venice. (Tretiakov Gallery, Moscow)

3. Portrait of Tsaritsa Natalia (mother of Peter I), 1680s. Oil on canvas, artist unknown. (Historical Museum, Moscow)

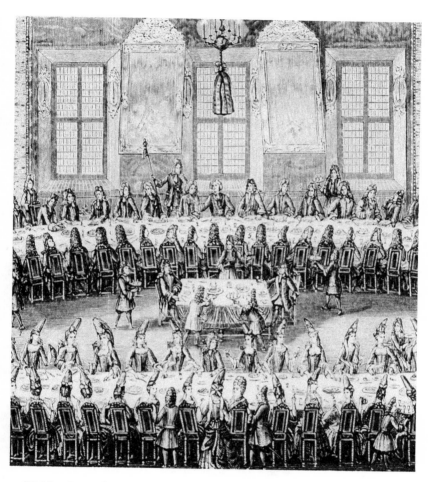

4. Wedding Feast of Peter and Catherine, 1712. Etching by Aleksei Zubov. The feast takes place amid the Baroque splendors of the new Winter Palace in St. Petersburg. Peter, dressed in naval uniform with the sash and star of his Order of St. Andrew, sits at the table center rear, looking forward. Catherine, wearing a stately wig and European court dress, sits center bottom, turning our way. (From A. G. Brikner, *Illustrirovaniiaia istoriia Petra Velikago*, St. Petersburg, 1882)

5. Carel de Moor, portrait of Tsaritsa Catherine (wife of Peter I), 1717. Oil on canvas. The portrait was painted from life at The Hague. Catherine is wearing the sash and star of the Order of St. Catherine. (Hermitage Museum, St. Petersburg)

6. "Peter the First, Emperor of the Russians." Engraving by Jacobus Houbraken, 1717, after the portrait in oil painted from life by Carel de Moor, 1717, at The Hague (see the companion portrait of wife Catherine at Fig. 5). (Author's collection)

7. Siege of Peter I's play citadel of "Pressburg" at Preobrazhenskoe, suburban Moscow. Early eighteenth-century drawing, artist unknown. (Historical Museum, Moscow)

8. Adriaan Schoonebeck, *Conquest of Azov in 1696*, 1699. Etching. Tsar Peter is pictured in Russian dress with sword on horseback surrounded by his officers, several in European dress, notably, in foreground, General Patrick Gordon. Peter's Austrian master of siegecraft stands before him pointing to a plan of the siegeworks. Also visible are the naval forces deployed in the successful Russian siege of the elaborate Ottoman fortifications. (From Brikner, *Illustrirovaniiaia istoriia*, 1882)

9. Warship of Peter I. Etching by A. Schoonebeck, 1701. (Rijksmuseum, Amsterdam)

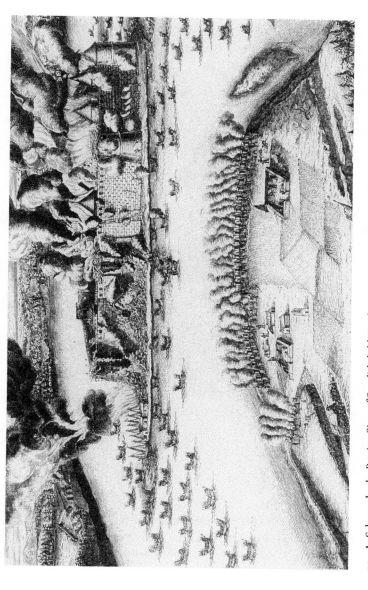

10. A. Schoonebeck, *Russian Siege of Swedish-held Noteborg in 1702*, 1703. Etching. Russian mastery under Peter I of the techniques of modern fortification and siegecraft, and of combined land and naval operations, is evident in this picture commissioned by Peter of an early Russian success in the Northern War. (From A. Brikner, *Illustrirovaniiaia istoriia*, 1882)

11. Portrait of Tsar Aleksei Mikhailovich (father of Peter I), 1672. Pen and watercolor on paper. Inscription in traditional Cyrillic script reads: "Tsar and Grand Prince Aleksei Mikhailovich of All Great and Little and White Russia Autocrat." (From N. V. Ustiugov et al., *Russkoe gosudarstvo v XVII veke: Sbornik statei,* Moscow, 1961, fig. 6)

12. Reception of Peter I by the boy-king Louis XV and his court, May 1717. Etching by F. Landry, published Paris, 1717. (Author's collection)

13. Portrait of "His Excellency Peter John Potemkin Ambassdr. Extraordinary from the Czar of Moscovy to His Majesty of Great Brittaine, in the Yeare 1682." Engraving by R. White after painting by Godfrey Kneller. Note the prominently displayed pelts and wild animals, symbolic of Muscovy's reputation as a supplier of animal skins to western Europe. (© Copyright The British Museum)

14. Portrait of A. A. Matveev. Engraving by N. Kolpakov, 1766, after portrait from life attributed to Hyacinthe Rigaud, Paris, 1705–1706. (Author's collection)

15. Main gates of the fortress (kremlin) of Rostov Veliky (Rostov the Great), 1670–1683, with Church of the Resurrection (1670) behind them. (Photograph by Jack E. Kollmann)

фиг. 1.

Перепопачальная С.Петербургская кртпость

16. Artist's reconstruction of (foreground) the first Peter-Paul church and fortress,
St. Petersburg. Mid-eighteenth-century Russian engraving. These wooden structures, contemporary European in design, were soon replaced by Dominico
Trezzini's masonry buildings, which, modified and expanded in later years, are
still standing. (From G. Bogdanov, *Istoricheskoe, geograficheskoe i topograficheskoe
opisanie Sanktpeterburga s 1703 po 1751 god*, ed. V. Ruban, St. Petersburg, 1779.
Houghton Library, Harvard University)

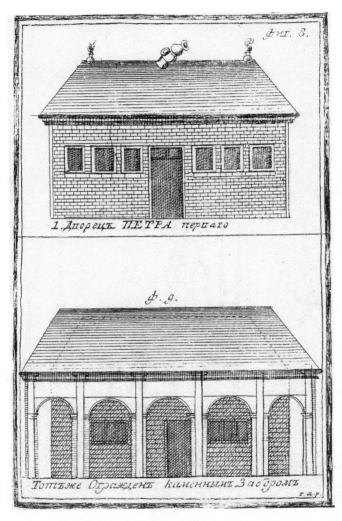

17. Mid-eighteenth-century Russian engraving of Peter I's *domik* and protective gallery, St. Petersburg. Note how the planed wooden walls have been painted, Dutch-style, to look like brick. (From Bogdanov, *Istoricheskoe, geograficheskoe i topograficheskoe opisanie Sanktpeterburga*)

18. Church of the Intercession of the Mother of God at Fili (now in Moscow),
1690–1693; detail of the upper tiers, combining Baroque motifs imported from
Europe with traditional Russian designs. (Photograph by the author)

19. View of Moscow from the south, across the Moscow river, ca. 1702. Engraving after drawing by Cornelis de Bruyn, a Dutch artist and explorer who traveled extensively in Russia between 1701 and 1707. (From de Bruyn, *Voyages par la Moscovie*, Amsterdam, 1718. Houghton Library, Harvard University)

20. View of a street in Moscow. Engraving in Adam Olearius, *Vermehrte Newe Beschreibung der Moscowitischen und Persischen Reyse* (Schleswig, 1656). Olearius was on mission in Moscow in the 1630s and again in 1643; this illustrated account of his visits went through numerous editions and translations in seventeenth-century Europe. (Regenstein Library, University of Chicago)

21. Images of Saints Peter and Paul from a widely used seventeenth-century Russian *podlinnik* or icon pattern book. (From *Stroganovskii ikonopisnyi litsevoi podlinnik*, Moscow, 1869. Harvard College Library)

22. Godfrey Kneller, portrait of Peter I, 1698. Oil on canvas. (The Royal Collection © 2003, Her Majesty Queen Elizabeth II)

23. Portrait of Peter I after Kneller (Fig. 22), attributed to I. Adolsky (Adol'skii), ca. 1700. Miniature in oil on enamel on copper base in silver frame. (Hermitage Museum, St. Petersburg)

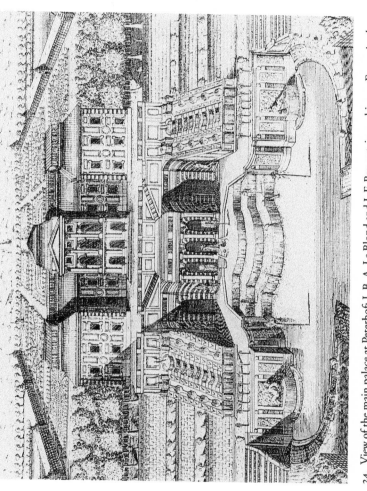

24. View of the main palace at Peterhof, J. B. A. Le Blond and J. F. Braunstein, architects. Engraving by Aleksei Zubov, 1717. Visible behind the palace is the Upper Park and, beneath the terrace in front, the grotto and cascade with pool and canal leading to the Finnish Gulf. (From I. N. Bozherianov, *Nevskii prospekt: kul'turno-istoricheskii ocherk*, 1901, p. 51)

Peter Alexèwitz, de groote Czàr
der Rüßen heeft dit met de naald
op koper geëtst, onder de directie van
Hadriaan Schooneleer, tot Amsterdam,
den 1698, in sin logie en slaap-
kamer, op de werf van de oostindische
maatschappy:

25. Allegory of the Russian victory over the Turks at Azov in 1696. Etching by Peter I,
1698. (Rijksmuseum, Amsterdam)

26. Obverse with portrait of Peter I of a new-style silver ruble minted in Moscow, 1720. (Author's collection)

27. Artist's reconstruction of traditional Cyrillic (Church Slavonic) alphabet of sixteenth–eighteenth centuries. (From L. Semenova, ed., *Shrifty*, Dmitrov, n.d., no. 1)

28. Peter I's "civil" alphabet of 1710. (From Semenova, ed., *Shrifty,* no. 12)

29. View of the interior of the Kunstkamera, St. Petersburg, 1718–1734; G. J. Mattarnowy, architect. Engraving by G. Kachalov, 1741. Visible here in section is (left) the Kunstkamera proper, or Peter I's collection of anatomical, anthropological, and historical exhibits; the central tower containing an anatomy theater, globe, and observatory; and (right) the Imperial Library. (Houghton Library, Harvard University)

30. A Russian village in 1930. While the houses are all built of logs, in traditional Russian fashion, their design along with the linear layout of the village itself can be traced directly to the Petrine revolution. (Official Soviet photograph, courtesy of Society for Cultural Relations with the U.S.S.R., London)

31. Russian peasants before a roadside icon, as drawn from life ca. 1790 and etched and printed by J. A. Atkinson, 1804. (Houghton Library, Harvard University)

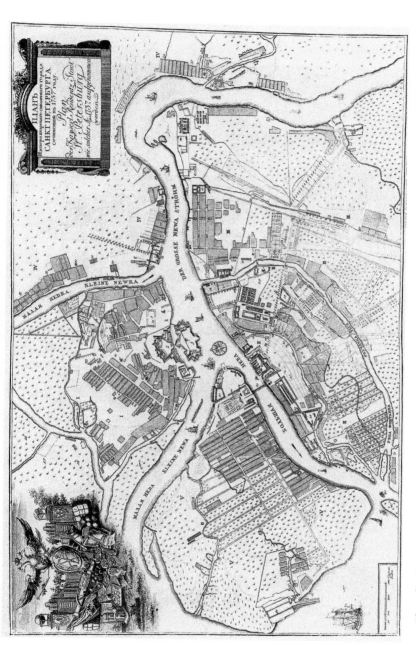

32. Plan of St. Petersburg, 1737. Engraving by G. I. Unvertzagt. (Author's collection)

33. Facade of the first Winter Palace, St. Petersburg, 1711; D. Trezzini, architect. Etching by Aleksei Zubov, 1717. Officials and courtiers, all in European dress, come and go by carriage and launch. (Hermitage Museum, St. Petersburg)

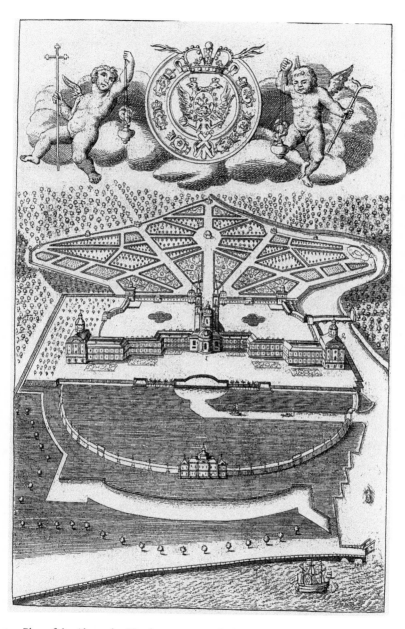

34. Plan of the Alexander-Nevsky monastery, St. Petersburg, as designed by
Dominico Trezzini. Engraving ca. 1732. (From A. de LaMottraye, *Voyages en divers
provinces,* The Hague, 1732. Regenstein Library, University of Chicago)

35. Palace of Kadriorg, Tallinn (formerly Reval), Estonia, 1718–1727; N. Michetti, architect. One of the few palaces to survive intact from the Petrine period. (Photograph by the author)

36. View of the Admiralty, St. Petersburg, with (far right) the second church (1717) of St. Isaac; G. J. Mattarnowy, architect. Engraving ca. 1730 attributed to O. Elliger after drawing by C. Marselius. (Houghton Library, Harvard University)

5

Revolution and Resistance

The most dramatic act of resistance to Peter's revolution in Russia was committed by his own son, Tsarevich Aleksei. His arrest, trial, and conviction for treason and rebellion against his father, and his death in the Peter-Paul fortress in St. Petersburg shortly thereafter (June 1718), were discussed in Chapter 1. There we saw that as early as January 1715 Peter had written to Aleksei charging him with intending to destroy whatever good his father had been able to do for his people should Aleksei succeed to the throne. Now it might be emphasized that while few people were convicted and punished for crimes allegedly committed in support of the tsarevich, the circle of his sympathizers appears to have been wide, and to have ranged from senior officials of both church and state to innumerable ordinary folk. Moreover, to judge from the available evidence—that published at the time as well as that since uncovered by historians—the goals of the disjointed "conspiracy" centering on Aleksei were to seize power on Peter's death, perhaps to hasten that event, and, once in power, to reverse the Petrine revolution.

The conspirators yearned, in their own words, to return to "the ancient customs and to live after the old ways." They dreamed of burning St. Petersburg to the ground, of destroying the navy, and of killing or banishing the many foreigners occupying senior positions in the tsar's service. No evidence of any concerted effort to achieve these goals has ever been uncovered. But Peter and his government, their supporters and friends, had good cause to be apprehensive anyway.

In fact, opposition in one form or another to Peter personally or to his policies was a continuous feature of his reign. His accession to the throne as a boy of ten was opposed by units of the royal musketeers *(streltsy)* who favored his half-brother, Ivan, and staged bloody riots in protest. Seven years later, in 1689, the same or other royal musketeers were involved in an attempted coup against the seventeen-year-old tsar instigated apparently by his half-sister Sophia, who had been acting as regent and was eager to remain in power. These events of his youth, during which Peter believed his life to be threatened, are thought to have made him acutely sensitive to any hint of opposition, and to have steeled his resolve to turn his "play soldiers" into the trusted guards regiments—the sovereign's "life guards"—that would form the core of his reorganized army. In the 1690s he assigned one of those regiments, the Preobrazhensky (it took its name from the royal estate of Preobrazhenskoe, near Moscow, where it was headquartered), to the basic garrison and police duties in Moscow formerly carried out by *streltsy,* whom he had every reason to distrust (and they, him). In 1696 he gave the headquarters of the regiment, the Preobrazhensky Office, jurisdiction over political offenses committed anywhere in Russia regardless of the offender's rank and regardless of where the case might already have been tried. It was the first office of political police ever established in Russia, and its creation may be said to mark the actual beginning of Peter's bureaucratic revolution.

The *streltsy* were malcontents and their grievances a perennial source of unrest for the monarchy. Founded in the 1550s by Ivan the Terrible as the first standing military force in the country, they had become progressively obsolete in the seventeenth century as new-style infantry units assumed an ever-larger role in Muscovite military campaigns. By the 1680s they were garrisoned in Moscow and a few frontier towns, where they had to perform, as mentioned, basic police duties as well as ceremonial guard functions. They were in addition poorly paid and poorly trained, and had taken to various trades to support themselves and their families. And their ranks were permeated by the traditionalist Muscovite religion, isolationist and apocalyptic, known as Old Belief. As a result of all these factors, they were easily inflamed and manipulated by politicians looking for a show of military support. Hence their part in the events of 1682 and 1689. In the 1680s and early 1690s, moreover, Tsar Peter pitted units of *streltsy* against his proto-guards regiments in his increasingly serious war games, a role that cannot have endeared him to them. Nor did their impressment for service as ordinary troops in the Azov campaigns of 1695–1696 win Peter their support.

But the capacity of the *streltsy* for making trouble was not yet at an end. In 1698 they staged a revolt while Peter was away on his Grand Embassy in Europe, a revolt that was swiftly put down by new-style regiments under the command of General Patrick Gordon. On his return to Moscow Peter launched a horrible reprisal, subjecting more than a thousand of the offenders to public torture and execution and disbanding the rest. Even then some former *streltsy* stationed at Astrakhan on the lower Volga mounted another revolt in the summer of 1705, ostensibly to protest the new regulations governing military dress. The rebels also sought to exploit local discontent over increased taxes and labor dues, and appealed for help to the local Cossacks, who were semi-independent frontiersmen and ever ready for a fight. "We stood up in Astrakhan for the Christian faith and against shaving and German dress and tobacco because we and our wives and children were not admitted into church in old Russian dress," the rebels declared to the Cossacks, going on to denounce the mock ceremonials enjoyed by Peter and company. "Instead of God-respecting carol singing they use masquerades and games, in which one of his courtiers, a jester, was given the title of patriarch, and others made archbishops." Peter's initially conciliatory efforts failed to win the rebels over, and regular troops spared from the current Baltic campaign stormed Astrakhan in March 1706. More than three hundred rebels were subsequently executed, most of them in Moscow after trial at the Preobrazhensky Office. Another forty-five died while under interrogation.[1]

The most serious revolt of a military nature against Peter's regime occurred in 1707–1708 and was led by disaffected Cossacks of the Don region under Kondraty Bulavin. Again, the grievances combined those particular to a special group of the tsar's subjects—in this case, alleged infringements by his government on traditional Don Cossack liberties and enterprises—with others of a more general nature, the latter including resentment of "German" influence at court, fear of being forced to shave one's beard, and outrage at rumored offenses committed by various grandees and their agents against the "true faith." It was a difficult moment for Peter in his war against Charles XII of Sweden, who at the beginning of 1708 invaded Russian territory. Bulavin and his Cossacks won support from Cossacks in southern Ukraine, from conscripted workers at the Voronezh shipyards and in the Azov area, from various indigenous tribes in the southeastern lands, and from Old Believers and fugitive serfs. Indeed, the whole affair looked like a replay of the rebellion led by Stenka Razin that had shaken the Muscovite state in the 1670s, or a preview of that led by Pugachev that would upset the Russian Empire in the 1770s. But now, as then and later, a large force of regular troops put down the rebellion, harsh punishments were meted out, and Peter's reputation for severity, as attested by folk songs from the time, was reinforced. Generally less serious outbreaks of sometimes violent protest against the taxes or conscriptions imposed by Peter's government occurred elsewhere in frontier areas during his reign and particularly in Ukraine, where in 1708 the Cossack leader Hetman Ivan Mazepa and several thousand followers renounced their allegiance to the tsar and joined forces with the Swedish invaders. Both were summarily defeated at the battle of Poltava in June 1709. But Peter retained ever after a deep suspicion of Ukrainian separatist pretensions, a suspicion that was generally reciprocated by Ukrainian leaders.[2]

After 1709 Peter was not confronted again by internal resistance of a mass or organized military nature, in part because of the prowess demonstrated by his forces at Poltava, in part because of his now legendary fame as a strong ruler. But domestic opposition of a more diffuse, individual kind persisted. The records of the Preobrazhensky Office contain evidence of such opposition starting in 1696, the year the office assumed jurisdiction over political offenses committed anywhere in the tsar's realm. One of the first such cases it investigated involved a priest named Avraamy, who had been a monk and then the abbot of a monastery outside Moscow that had become a center, owing to his presence there, for mendicants and pilgrims of all social ranks. Peter had visited Avraamy's monastery as a child, and the good monk's interest in public affairs and in the new learning seeping in from the west had recommended him to the young tsar, who invited him to join his company on their sailing expedition of 1688. But by the late 1690s, reflecting on the first years of Peter's personal rule, Avraamy was a troubled man, and had the courage and the compassion for his equally troubled flock to say so openly. In January 1697 he advised Peter in writing that people were unhappy with his reign so far, that instead of busying himself with state affairs he had indulged in actions "displeasing to God," that when he had married everyone had hoped he would become "like a mature man, whence all would be governed for the better." But Peter had continued to devote himself to "unseemly and unnecessary games," and instead of an auspicious start to his reign he had produced widespread sadness and grief by his "ridiculous talk and pranks and acts displeasing to God." According to Avraamy, there was serious doubt abroad as to whether any good could come of this reign, and so he was laying before the tsar this reminder of his heavy duties as judge and ruler, strongly implying that the delays and inefficiency and even corruption in the government were due to Peter's neglect and personal conduct. Avraamy concluded by warning that many felt as he did but were afraid to complain openly. In his opinion, the time had come "and the hour [had] drawn nigh when these evils must be shunned and good deeds begun."

For his pains Avraamy was arrested, taken to the Preobrazhensky Office, interrogated about his informants, and then banished to a distant monastery (from which he continued nonetheless to write to Peter). Meanwhile, the tsar's political police were also investigating Ivan Tsykler, a Moscow nobleman and former colonel of musketeers who had recently been put in charge of building port facilities at Taganrog, near Azov. He was accused of plotting to depose Peter in favor of his little son Aleksei, with Sophia acting again as regent (or perhaps to replace Peter as tsar with a more sympathetic grandee), this because of Peter's treatment of the *streltsy* and other seemingly outrageous measures, like planning to send noblemen's sons abroad for study. In March 1697 Tsykler and several fellow conspirators with both musketeer and Old Believer affiliations were executed. Other conspirators were beaten, deprived of their status and property, and/or exiled. And with this and the case of Avraamy thus disposed of, Peter went off on his prolonged Grand Embassy to Europe, a prospect so novel—the tsar of holy Moscow going west to the lands of the Latin schismatics and Protestant heretics for an indefinite stay— that it alone filled the Tsykler conspirators, they had confessed, with profound dread.[3]

Systematic study of the records of the Preobrazhensky Office from 1696 to 1725 indicates that about 5 percent of the several thousand cases brought before it involved noblemen, another 5 percent *streltsy,* about 20 percent clergy, and the rest—70 percent—ordinary peasants and townsfolk. The crimes of which they stood accused included acts of outright rebellion (by the *streltsy* in 1698 and the Astrakhan and Bulavin rebels in 1705–1706 and 1707–1708), espionage (at Azov in 1696), threats against the tsar's life, pretensions to his throne, despoiling his image, distorting his titles, and abusing his name. They also included expressions of support or even of sympathy for the deposed regent, Sophia, or for Peter's first wife, Evdokia, who had been banished to a convent in 1698. Other such "unseemly utterances" touched not only on Peter, his personal conduct, or his relations with his company but also on his second wife, Catherine, their children, other members of the royal family, and leading figures of the regime like Prince Menshikov.

Following the trial and death of Aleksei in 1718 expressions of support or even of sympathy for the late tsarevich were added to the list of political offenses prosecuted both by the Preobrazhensky Office, near Moscow, and by the Secret Chancellery in St. Petersburg. The latter had been created to investigate the Aleksei affair and, between 1718 and 1725, it tried another 370 "grave matters" brought before it, often by Peter himself. In 1722 the Holy Synod, which by the terms of the *Ecclesiastical Regulation* of 1721 had replaced the patriarchate at the head of the church, added a provision to the *Regulation* requiring priests to report to one of these offices anything they had heard in confession that smacked of treason. More, in a supplementary Announcement to the clergy of May 1722, also prepared with Peter's personal participation, the Synod recounted several "actual cases" that justified, it said, the provision requiring priests in effect to violate the traditional and canonical secrecy of confession.

These cases offer further evidence of the nature and extent of domestic opposition to Peter's regime. One had arisen in the course of Tsarevich Aleksei's trial (1718), when it was discovered that "during confession he [Aleksei] had told his confessor that he wished his father were dead; and this confessor forgave him in the name of God and said that he too wished he were dead, which this former confessor himself admitted under interrogation . . . and for this evil deed he [the confessor] was put to a well-deserved death." A second case had come to trial earlier in 1722 because, the Synod went on to report,

> a certain malefactor, on arrival in the town of Penza, publicly uttered many evil things against His Most Illustrious Imperial Majesty [Peter], and most pernicious words against the State, about which an inquisition is now under way in the Secret Chancellery. But from this inquisition it has already appeared that this malefactor had intimated these evil words to his priest in confession, who did not in any way forbid them but indeed assented to some of them, as now this unfrocked priest himself has confessed under interrogation.

The "malefactor" in question was later executed, essentially for the crime of calling Peter the Antichrist. His trial also resulted in the informal trial by the Holy Synod of its own president, Stefan Yavorsky, a distinguished senior cleric from the Ukraine, who was alleged to have remarked to the defendant that Peter was not the Antichrist but an "iconoclast"—a contemporary Orthodox euphemism for Protestant.

A third such case cited by the Synod in its Announcement of 1722 concerned "the criminal Talitsky," who

> intimated to his priest in confession his most wicked intention, namely, to write a letter by means of which he wished everywhere to incite sedition, insisting that it was right and not to be forsaken; and the priest, although this [intention] disgusted him, nevertheless gave him communion, and did not report it to the appropriate authorities . . . and this criminal proceeded to carry out his criminal intention. And

should he not have been caught in the act, what blood and disasters would have issued therefrom! And to what wickedness the sacrament of penance had been put by Talitsky and his confessor!

The records of the Preobrazhensky Office show that Talitsky was tried and executed in 1700–1701 for composing a leaflet in which the proximate end of the world was predicted, Moscow was called Babylon, Peter was denounced as the Antichrist, and the people were bidden not to serve the tsar or pay his taxes. Talitsky apparently had planned, with a following thus aroused and with the help of disaffected musketeers, to depose Peter while he was away on campaign and to replace him with a certain, presumably sympathetic, boyar. Seventeen persons were named by Talitsky as his supporters and summoned to the Preobrazhensky Office; five, including two priests, were executed after interrogation, eight were condemned to flogging, mutilation, and banishment to Siberia, and one, the bishop of Tambov, was deposed and banished to a monastery in the far north. The case was cited in a secret admonition to the clergy issued by Peter in 1708, at the height of the Bulavin rebellion, and in an official admonition to religious dissenters of January 1722, as well as in the Synod's Announcement of May of that year. In the eyes of Peter and his supporters, it would seem, Talitsky had come to personify all who opposed his regime.[4]

In short, the evidence of opposition to Peter contained in official records, foreign ambassadors' reports, religious writings, folklore, and other contemporary sources is abundant. But what does this evidence tell us about motives or causes? It reveals, for a start, that much of Peter's opposition derived from what might be called built-in or longstanding sources of grievance and discontent. Such would include the belligerence of the royal musketeers, whose progressive obsolescence Peter did nothing to alleviate but rather, committed as he was to wholesale military modernization, did everything to hasten, at first by marginalizing or even disbanding them as a standing force and then, when they rebelled, by harshly, even brutally repressing them. Such built-in opposition would also include, to take another clear instance, the hostility of the courtiers displaced by Peter's counter-coup of 1689, most conspicuously the former regent Sophia and her relatives, clients, and friends, whose fall from positions of power and wealth was precipitous. The acts of venal or incompetent officials that incited some recorded acts of opposition to Peter's regime would fall into this category, too; such acts were habitual in Muscovite government, to some degree in governments everywhere, and were plainly beyond even Peter's power to eliminate, try as he periodically did.

Equally, the many complaints of Old Believers, rooted as they were in the church schism of the 1660s, were directed mainly against the official church and only then against any ruler who supported it—as any ruler would and did, from Peter's father on. In fact, while initially continuing his predecessors' policy of persecuting overt manifestations of Old Belief among his subjects (certain ways of crossing themselves, of saying their prayers, and so on), Peter eventually moderated the policy to one of limited toleration in exchange for loyalty and the payment of special taxes or fines. But the age-old burdens of serfdom, which continued to cause complaint, some of it serious enough to be investigated by the Preobrazhensky Office, were nowise alleviated by Peter's government. Instead, his new taxes and increased military and labor conscriptions in pursuit of his wars and building projects only augmented the burdens borne by the peasantry, whose grievances in this respect remained a source of popular discontent long thereafter. We should also note that this more general or built-in opposition to Peter was not only active but passive, that it often took the form of flight or evasion, as the tsar's army recruiters, tax collectors, and special inspectors constantly complained. To the many opponents of Peter formally prosecuted by his government, in other words, we can add the countless more of his subjects who protested by hiding from his officials, by hoodwinking them, or simply by vanishing.

The evidence in question also reveals that many of Peter's opponents were specifically motivated by hostility to his innovations, especially those touching on dress and religion. Such opponents denounced his promotion of practices like smoking tobacco, shaving the beard, wearing "German" clothes and hairstyles, including wigs, and adopting the common European calendar (albeit in its Julian or Old-Style form, which in the eighteenth century was eleven days behind the Gregorian or New-Style calendar that was already superseding it). According to this calendar, the year was calculated from the birth of Christ and began on January 1, while by the Byzantine calendar long used in Russia the year was calculated "from the creation of the world" (which supposedly happened in 5509 B.C.) and began on September 1, which was thus a major holiday. By decree of Peter in 1699 (or 7208 according to the traditional calculation), a new year as well as a new century was to begin in Russia on January 1, 1700, an event that was to be celebrated with "appropriate festivities."[5]

All of Peter's measures affecting dress and personal appearance, holidays and the calendar, were part and parcel of his increasingly ambitious program of cultural Europeanization—of bringing Russian cultural practices into conformity with those commonly followed in Europe. As such they invariably provoked resistance among the groups most affected, seeming as they did to violate, without adequate or clear justification (which Peter sometimes tried to provide), longstanding Russian customs and prohibitions. Not surprisingly, the terms in which this resistance was expressed were those of traditional Russian culture (what else?): religious, patriotic, apocalyptic, uncompromising. Nor were the grievances thus expressed unconnected with others of a more strictly economic or political nature, as also indicated above. In short, Peter's many cultural innovations were at once the cause of, and an excuse for, much of the opposition to his regime.

The old Muscovite nobility and the clergy of the Russian Orthodox church certainly had plenty to complain about in Peter's
time, and so it is not surprising that the opposition of these two
groups, especially the clergy, seems to have been disproportion-
ately larger than their actual numbers in society. Russia before
Peter had been ruled by its tsar but always in conjunction with a
cohort of senior nobles. The nobles in turn dominated the subordinate offices and military forces of the tsar's government, offices
and forces that were run and largely manned by their kinsmen
and clients. Conflict with more modern European armies was rendering the traditional noble cavalry increasingly obsolete well
before Peter took control. Even so, the enserfment of the nobles'
peasants and de facto hereditary possession of their lands (rather
than possession in return for military service) had been granted
by the tsar's government over the course of the seventeenth century. Peter disrupted this cozy system, as we have seen, essentially
by drafting the entire nobility into lifetime state service in return
for government salaries and perquisites and secure possession of
their lands (exemptions from service were allowed only in cases of
dire necessity—for example, when the only son of a widowed
mother was needed to run the family estate). He also decreed
that only one heir could inherit a noble estate, thus disrupting the
custom of partible inheritance whereby parents provided lands
for all their children, male and female, who would thereby retain
noble landowning status. Yet more, state service had been made
newly burdensome by Peter's insistence on acquiring appropriate technical education, even at the hands of foreigners, and on
making promotion contingent on merit. Foreigners—people of
other faiths speaking strange tongues—now also filled, not always
temporarily, most of the senior ranks in the army and navy. No
wonder the evidence of noble dissatisfaction under Peter is extensive. He also dismantled the traditional apparatus of government, replacing it with a system of central and local offices—
his bureaucratic revolution—in which the same principles of

appropriate education and promotion by merit were supposed to prevail.

What was a nobleman of traditional Muscovite upbringing and expectations now to do? He could not stay home on his country estate, a little tsar in his own world, but had to report to Moscow or St. Petersburg for military or naval training in one of the new technical schools in preparation for a career in which promotion and the rewards that went with it were by no means assured. A steady and eventually successful struggle by the nobility for restoration of partible inheritance and for emancipation from compulsory state service ensued: Peter's law on single inheritance was repealed in 1730 and his system of compulsory service was abolished in 1762.[6] In the meantime, somewhat ironically, the attractions of state service, especially in the higher ranks, the financial rewards and social prestige to be gained thereby, made it increasingly important for most noblemen (let alone aspiring nobles) to spend a considerable portion of their lives in state service.

Similarly, the traditional autonomy and privileges of the clergy were drastically curtailed by Peter. In suspending and then abolishing the patriarchate and replacing it with a governing board—the Holy Synod—of senior clerics appointed by him, he in effect incorporated the administration of the church in his newly reorganized state. He also insisted on newly rigorous standards of education for the clergy so that they could both better perform their traditional duties and take on newly imposed ones, like registering the vital statistics of all their parishioners—their births (baptisms), marriages, and deaths—and reporting religious dissidence or other suspicious political behavior to the appropriate government offices. In pursuit of the relevant provisions of the *Ecclesiastical Regulation* of 1721, schools were created in every diocese for the mandated training of clergy. Parish priests were also obliged to read to their congregations and then to post in their churches all official announcements and decrees. The number of monastic clergy—monks and nuns living in monasteries and convents—was to be sharply curtailed, and they too were to take on new responsibilities, such as caring for retired soldiers and weaving linen for sailcloth. The number of secular clergy—priests and others serving in parishes—was to be restricted to those who actually served as such, and the immunity of both secular and monastic clergy from prosecution for violations of the civil or criminal laws (their right to be tried in special church courts) was virtually abolished.

Some priests, monks, and bishops made known their opposition to these changes in their status and governance by preaching more or less pointed sermons, drawing on traditional Orthodox or even Roman Catholic teachings about the rights of the church. Others openly condemned the presence of foreigners in favored positions or directly criticized Peter, as we have seen, some going so far as to call him Antichrist. Thus it is little wonder that clergy constituted some 20 percent of all the political cases tried during Peter's reign at the Preobrazhensky Office, though they constituted no more than 2 percent of the total population. At the same time, we should also note that at least some of the clergy actively embraced the Petrine church reform with its emphasis on education and service, and that with the expansion of clerical education thereafter the Russian Orthodox church eventually became the most learned branch of Eastern Orthodoxy. When viewed historically, in other words, Peter's record with respect to both the nobility and the clergy of Russia contains decidedly positive or progressive elements as well as negative or regressive ones.

Much of Peter's opposition, to be sure, was aroused by his own "unseemly" or abusive behavior. It was aroused, as the records repeatedly indicate, by his smoking and drinking and carousing in public, by his often shabby or foreign or otherwise unregal dress, by his frequent indulgence in extravagant jokes and pranks, often at the expense of the church and its rites, by his divorce from his first wife and then remarriage to a lowly foreigner, and by his treatment of his son and erstwhile heir, Tsarevich Aleksei. Much of Peter's opposition, in other words, was provoked by his perpetual, public, and seemingly unconcerned revelation of the many follies, vices, and frailties of the tsar himself, hitherto a sacrosanct figure in Russian society. Indeed, the most common complaint brought against Peter's regime, the common thread running through the endless denunciations lodged at the Secret Chancellery or at the Preobrazhensky Office, cutting across rank and social condition, was that in his personal conduct as much as in his policies Peter had revealed himself to be a false tsar. He was a "tyrant" or "imposter," "Antichrist" or the "servant of Antichrist," really a "German" or a "Swede" in disguise, a "heretic," "blasphemer," or "iconoclast." It is easy to dismiss these epithets as the rantings of simpletons, ignoring the accusations embedded in them. It is also easy to describe their focus on the person of the tsar as naive monarchism, forgetting its cultural matrix—forgetting, in both instances, the limited conceptual and linguistic resources available to Peter's opponents. Historians now know better than to take such a dismissive approach.[7]

Interwoven with all or most of the recorded expressions of opposition to Peter's regime, in sum, was a largely spontaneous cultural reaction to a largely imposed cultural revolution. Modes of dress and personal behavior, ways of depicting God, his Mother, and the saints, the governance of the church, the alphabet and the calendar, the image of the ruler, the roles in society of both clergy and nobility, the location and appearance of the country's capital, the operations of government, the organization of the armed forces, the tax and monetary systems—all these areas of public and even private life had undergone more or less drastic change, all as mandated by the ruler and his agents in the space of two, or at most three, decades. Such a sudden displacement of familiar, customary ways of doing things in favor of what had been previously unknown, feared, or scorned could not have been a simple, inconsequential matter in a traditional, minimally literate society like Muscovite Russia. On the contrary, both the frequency and the extremity of society's reactions to various of these changes are a measure of just how drastic they were. Among Russians even centuries later the Petrine revolution, despite its positive outcomes, still evoked criticism precisely for its sudden, sweeping, and coercive character.[8]

The cultural essence, so to speak, of the Petrine revolution was discussed in the preceding chapter. There, changes in architectural norms and techniques and then in the whole Russian built world came first—setting the stage, as we might call it now. Next came the wholesale changes in imagery implanted in Russia by Peter along with the new techniques of image-making: the scenery, props, and costumes left by him to fill the stage of the new Russia built by his architectural revolution. Then came the verbal revolution, producing the scripts to be spoken or read by the actors destined to tread that stage. In short, the theater of Russian life, especially of upper-class Russian life centered on the Imperial court, had been transformed. But this metaphor, apposite as it may at first seem, oversimplifies the revolution's complex history as recounted, even then in greatly digested form, in the rest of this book. The new ways of building, visualizing, and verbalizing were only gradually assimilated by the rank-and-file of the official-noble elite, for one thing, and still more gradually so by the townsfolk and peasants who made up the bulk of society. The metaphor may also lead readers to think that with the death of Peter in 1725 the revolution was over and done with; that the resistance in Russia to wholesale Europeanization and the modernization it entailed thus died, too, and with it old Muscovy. Such was not, most emphatically, the case.

The persistence of old Muscovy, together with or in spite of the Europeanized Russia of Peter the Great, took many forms. In architecture, wood remained the favorite building material over most of Russia until well into the twentieth century (Fig. 30), although the traditional techniques and styles of building in wood were gradually displaced by more modern ones (the axe by the saw, simple log construction by frame, bark or sod roofs by shingles, small unglazed apertures by windows paned with glass, traditional decorative forms by vaguely Baroque or Classical ones). Even then a nostalgia for traditional wooden forms periodically animated architectural revivals in Russia, and persists to this day, as may be seen particularly in the dachas, or country cottages, built by numerous urban Russians. Church architecture similarly resisted a stylistic takeover by the new norms emanating from St. Petersburg, as did icon painting and the language of church services, which remained Church Slavonic. Various Old Believer offshoots of the official church were especially conservative in these respects. The variegated and circuitous way in which the new imagery of the Petrine elite only gradually penetrated the folk art of Russia was also mentioned in Chapter 4. Still more telling, perhaps, was the coexistence in Russia until well into the twentieth century of distinct if interrelated verbal cultures, literate and oral, the one as codified in the standard Russian literary language that goes back to Peter, the other as spoken in a regionally variable *patois* or set of dialects that was rooted in the most distant Russian past and retained any number of pre-Petrine words and forms. Muscovy's cultural survival, that is to say, was obvious in the very language spoken by a great many Russians until very recently.

The persistence of what we might call Muscovite linguistic elements, like that of the purely folk elements in Russian vernacular art and architecture, was aided and abetted by the persistence over large areas of the country of "backward" social and economic conditions. Until well into the twentieth century the majority of Russians lived in rural isolation, working the land in largely self-sufficient village communities. Their culture was a peasant, still mainly oral culture, one that by the standards of the Europeanized elite was saturated with traditional patriarchal and religious values and expressed in often archaic or obsolete speech (Fig. 31). Russian peasant culture incorporated political, religious, social, economic, and personal attitudes and practices that were generally viewed by successive educated elites as, in a word, "primitive" (some educated Russians, by contrast, tended to idealize peasant society, seeing in it the survival of the "real," pre-Petrine Russia).[9] Moreover, the persistence of this age-old peasant culture was powerfully reinforced by the persistence of serfdom, which was legally liquidated only between 1861 and 1881. For centuries serfdom had ensnared half the rural population of Russia or more in habits of deference, servility, and petty cultivation. It was a world that in its vital and moral essentials remained largely untouched by the secularizing, aggrandizing, cosmopolitan imperatives of the Petrine revolution.

Peasant Russia has attracted a good deal of attention from historians, Russian and foreign, since the late nineteenth century.[10] One of the best such studies ever published, and arguably the best book on Russian history ever written by an American, is Geroid T. Robinson's *Rural Russia under the Old Regime*, which first appeared in 1932. It is the work of a sympathetic, well-informed outside observer, his sympathy rooted in his own rural origins in the United States and his observations informed by years of archival and library research and by traveling in Russia in the 1920s, when traditional peasant life was still largely intact. The book focuses on the Russian countryside between the serf emancipation of 1861 and what Robinson called the "agrarian revolution" of 1917. And at one point he writes:

The traveler of our own day who has journeyed across-country in Russian peasant wagons; watched the plowing, harvesting, and threshing; eaten from the common bowl, heard the peasant songs, and felt the rhythm of the peasant dances, can hardly help but think of the Russian village as a world apart; and yet times have changed, and already at the end of the nineteenth century many influences were at work to break the circle of the peasants' isolation.

These "many influences" stemmed, of course, from the emancipation proclaimed in 1861 and its multifarious aftermath, until which time

the village had not ceased to be the chief repository of the past: there was ample evidence that this was so, in the primitive land-system [of communal rather than individual tenure]; in the organization of the household and the commune; in the peasant folk-lore, with its occasional traces of a paganism officially abandoned nearly a thousand years ago; in the material arts, which still created many a fine thing in the old tradition.

Yet even with the advances in popular education and literacy of the decades succeeding serf emancipation and the concurrent growth of peasant landownership, even as "the Church, the conscript army, the school, and the press all helped to wear down the cultural isolation of the village," even while industrialization and urbanization were transforming parts of the Russian Empire, drawing some peasants away from the land and increasing the productivity, and improving the methods, of those who remained; even then

a pre-war [pre-1914] traveler from the United States would still have been strongly impressed by what might be called the mature and complex primitiveness of Russian peasant agriculture. It was not the primitiveness of pioneering; not new and raw, but stained and weathered, and worn round by time; not the beginning of a new history so much as some late chapter of an old one. All about, in the compact village, in the intricate pattern of the fields, in the routine of the seeding and the harvest, there were the evidences of a venerable tradition.

Robinson wrote after the 1917 revolution had at last "brought in the peasants to possess the land," all of the land, but before the catastrophe of Soviet collectivization had descended on rural Russia, destroying forever its traditional ways.[11]

Robinson did not neglect to research, and to observe the remnants of, that other social component of rural Russia in the post-Petrine period, the noble landlords living in their European "nests of gentility" scattered across the countryside, all summarily dispossessed by the revolution of 1917.[12] Indeed, his book begins by depicting one such "nest" he personally encountered while traveling in the south-central steppe in the fall of 1926:

> Against a horizon of rolling fields, banded black, green, and yellow with strips of fresh-plowed earth, sprouting winter grain, and fallowed stubble, there appeared a formal block of tree-tops; then, eventually, a keeper's cottage, and the wide gateway of a park. Walled here from the casual *step* [steppe, or great plain], was a deliberately conventional grove, now very much bedraggled; and beyond, facing upon a broad crescent of brambles, stood the wreck of a manor-house— one of those classical structures that speak so clearly of the wealth and the self-conscious culture of the nobility of the old regime.

Robinson was moved by the sight of "these architectural bones" to muse about the life that had been lived there, a life he subsequently documents in his book:

> . . . *troikas* at the door; bearded servants bowing and scraping; harpsichords and hunting feasts; the gossip of St. Petersburg and Paris; hoopskirts, silks and sabres; medaled dignitaries with powdered wigs, or the mutton-chop whiskers of a later day; daughters in French gowns, home from the

Riviera; sons in the Guards' uniform of the Napoleonic Wars or the Great War [World War I]—all musty and remote, buried more deeply by these last ten years [1916–1926] than by the ten decades that went before. [13]

We have come a long way from great Peter. Or have we? Robinson's emphasis on the huge distance Russia had traveled in the decade after 1916 would later be lost sight of by commentators struggling to comprehend the damage done to Russia in the 1930s and 1940s by Stalinism and World War II. The scope of these later catastrophes would somehow swallow up those of World War I and the Bolshevik revolution of 1917 in a continuous cascade of disaster for which some ultimate historical cause had to be found. Thus at least one prominent Russian historian writing in the 1980s ascribed to the legacy of Peter not only much that is modern in Russian history in a positive or progressivist sense, but also much that is somehow negative or disreputable, from the persistence of serfdom and the failures of capitalism to the calamity of 1917 and the ensuing "totalitarianism" of Stalin.[14] In this view, one might as well blame Russia's involvement in World War I if not in World War II on Peter, who had made Russia a major European power. The indictment is obviously exaggerated, if not unhistorical. Yet it is in its way a tribute to the magnitude and complexity over the longer term of the revolution led by Peter, where Russia's modern history unquestionably begins. It also suggests that the challenges posed by the Petrine revolution in Russia—how to Europeanize, but without losing Russian identity; how to modernize, but in a consensual, democratic way—are still far from fully resolved. Indeed, with the collapse of the Soviet experiment their resolution seems all the more urgent.

6

St. Petersburg

No major city of the modern world is more closely connected with its founder than St. Petersburg is with Peter. In so saying we invoke not just the various buildings that date directly from his time, which include the central fortress with its church of Saints Peter and Paul, where he is buried; his *domik,* or the little Dutch-style house that was his first home in the city, and is now a museum; the Summer Palace, built for him in 1710–1712 by Dominico Trezzini, a place so carefully preserved, in the words of a seasoned American specialist, that "one can actually feel Peter's presence"; and suburban Peterhof, as he called it (later russified to *Petrodvorets*), the complex of palaces and parks overlooking the Finnish Gulf that was his favorite retreat.[1] Nor do we confine ourselves to the many other buildings in St. Petersburg whose origins go back to his reign: the Winter Palace, the Admiralty, the Academy of Sciences, the Kunstkamera, the Menshikov palace, and the Building of the Twelve Colleges, the last erected to house the administrative colleges created in conjunction with Peter's bureaucratic revolution and now part of St. Petersburg University. Nor are we simply thinking of the many other mementos of Russia's first emperor to be found in the city—museum exhibits, historic sites, shop signs, street names, and monumental statues, including, most famously, the statue of Peter known as the Bronze Horseman, which was erected in his honor by Catherine II and later celebrated in a long poem of that name by Alexander Pushkin, who is often called Russia's greatest poet. Nor is it the popular nickname in Russian for St. Petersburg, "Piter," from the Dutch form of Peter's name (Pieter) that he liked to use when corresponding with members of his company. These elements of St. Petersburg today all constitute tangible links with Peter, to be sure; all are enduring reminders of his life and reign. But more important than any or all of them is the fact that in both its origins and its subsequent history St. Petersburg embodied the Petrine revolution. The whole city has an enduring historical significance, in other words, that goes well beyond its connections with the person of its founder.

Consider, for a start, its very site (Fig. 32). St. Petersburg's location, on a low-lying marshy delta, where the Neva river empties into the Finnish Gulf of the Baltic Sea, is the northernmost of any major city in the world. Its damp, raw climate is both unsettled and unsettling—the sun never fully rises in the depths of winter, never fully sets in high summer, creating its famed "white nights" of June and early July. The Neva and its tributaries regularly overflow, for an average of nearly one serious flood a year since the city's founding. The soils of the immediate area are poor, its vegetation sparse; under a natural economy it never supported more than a few fishing hamlets. Climate and location, with their recurrent mists and looming clouds, lend St. Petersburg that eerie or magical atmosphere hauntingly evoked by generations of local writers, painters, and poets. But a less auspicious setting in which to found the capital of a great empire, and a *Russian* empire at that, is hard to imagine.

There was no one act by or date on which St. Petersburg was founded, to be sure; it became the new capital by stages, as events and Peter's revolutionary project unfolded. First came the war with Sweden, which was basically motivated by the longstanding desire of Muscovy's rulers to gain, or regain, a foothold on the Baltic. Such had been the aim of the long and ultimately unsuccessful Livonian War waged more than a century before Peter's reign by Tsar Ivan IV (Ivan the Terrible), whose failure was well known to Peter; so was that of his own father's much more modest effort in the same direction. Peter's war began in the fall of 1700 with his unsuccessful, indeed disastrous siege of Narva, an old river port near the Finnish Gulf located about 160 kilometers west of the site that became St. Petersburg. Quickly regrouping and reequipping his forces, Peter ordered small-scale attacks on other Swedish strongholds positioned along the gulf. In 1702 he launched a major campaign from the north and east, making tactical use of Lake Ladoga, the source of the Neva and the largest lake in Europe, whose eastern shores were under Russian control. (Russians would make similar use of the lake in World War II when defending St. Petersburg, then known as Leningrad, against the long German siege.) In the spring of 1703 Russian forces captured the trading settlement called Nyenskans in Swedish (Nevalinna in Finnish), located just south of the last big bend in the Neva, where it turns west to flow rapidly into its delta. With its modern fort and outworks, its approximately 450 houses and Swedish, German, and Russian churches, it was the nearest settlement of any size to the site where St. Petersburg would rise. On or about May 2, 1703, Peter renamed the settlement Shlotburg (from German *Schlot,* or "neck," referring no doubt to the nearby neck of the Neva) and then went in search of a better place to fortify. He soon found a little island located about four kilometers down river from Shlotburg, in the main channel of the Neva, roughly at the point where it separates into several branches, a spot accessible from the gulf to the largest vessels then afloat. There, on May 16, the foundations of a fortress were laid. It was to be called, after the tsar's patron saint, St. Petersburg (*Sant-Piterburkh,* eventually *Sankt-Peterburg*), a typically Petrine Germanism (or Dutchism).

This date, May 16, 1703, came to mark the foundation of the city (or May 27, 1703 New Style).

In other words, it is clear from what evidence we have that the site of St. Petersburg was chosen for urgent tactical reasons, and that the city began life as a fortress. On June 29, 1703, a church was inaugurated within the fortress and dedicated to Saints Peter and Paul, whose feast day it was; the adjective, Peter-Paul *(petropavlovskaia)*, was eventually applied to the fortress itself. In various documents of the time Peter and his officials were soon referring to the ensemble of fortress, church, and attached encampment of soldiers and builders as "Petropolis" or "Petropol" as well as "St. Petersburg," names that similarly evoked a European aura. An issue of the Moscow *Gazette* published in August 1703 announced that "His Tsarist Majesty has ordered a fortified settlement to be built not far from Shlotburg, by the sea, so that henceforth all goods arriving [from Europe] should find a haven there, as should Persian and Chinese goods."[2]

The announcement indicates that Peter now had it in mind to create a major port at the site, too. In fact, the first friendly foreign ship, a Dutch merchantman, arrived in November 1703 with a cargo of salt and wine. Its captain was handsomely rewarded, and similar rewards were promised to others willing to venture up the gulf, past Swedish warships, to help supply the new Russian outpost. In 1704 Peter's forces finally captured Narva, giving him greater control of the approaches to St. Petersburg. In a letter to Menshikov of September 1704 he referred to the infant settlement as a "metropolis [*stolitsa*]," a Russian word that can also be translated as "capital" or "capital city." That same autumn construction began on an "admiralty [*admiralteistvo,* from Dutch *admiraliteit*]" or fortified shipyard situated on the left or southern bank of the Neva, just across and a little down river from the Peter-Paul fortress.

Thus within a year or so of its founding the fortress at the mouth of the Neva had been transformed in Peter's mind into a naval base as well, and more: into a potential port and major city. Yet before he could seriously proceed with any such plans an end to the war with Sweden had to be negotiated and the fate of his grandiose building projects at Azov resolved. Did he intend to build a new "Petropolis" on both the Baltic and the Black Seas? The issue would be decided not by Peter and his company in peaceful contemplation of their options but by the course of war. Steadfastly refusing to negotiate with the tsar and deciding, instead, to invade his territory with the aim of dethroning him, the Swedish king was roundly defeated by Russian forces at Poltava, in the Ukraine, in 1709; and two years later, at the battle by the Pruth, in Moldavia, Peter was obliged to capitulate to the much larger army of the Turkish grand vizier, which meant the end of his Petropolis in the south. He interpreted these two developments as Providential proof that he should focus his energies on securing his foothold on the Baltic and on building his "paradise," as he had begun to call it, in the north. By 1714 the construction of St. Petersburg so preoccupied him that he ordered an indefinite halt to any masonry construction anywhere else in his realm.

The Northern War between Russia and Sweden was not brought to an end until 1721 (the Peace of Nystad)—until Swedish forces had been soundly defeated at sea (1714), the Swedish warrior king, Charles XII, killed in battle (1718), and the Swedish homeland itself threatened with invasion. But meanwhile Peter hastened the buildup of St. Petersburg (and of his Baltic fleet), sparing no expense, the scale of the project seeming to grow ever grander from year to year. Such figures as we have indicate that between 1703 and 1725 anywhere from 10,000 to 30,000 workers labored annually on the construction of the city, their efforts directed by the thousand or more architects, masons, and interior decorators (plasterers, sculptors, woodcarvers) recruited for the purpose in Italy, Germany, Holland, and France. The first of the architects to arrive and in many ways the most important was Dominico Trezzini, who had been hired away from the Danish king's service in 1703 and was promptly dispatched, on reaching Moscow, to the site only recently named St. Petersburg. There he worked continuously until his death in 1734, building the city's first permanent fortifications (Fig. 16), laying out its streets and squares, designing and directing the construction of churches, palaces, and houses (Fig. 33), and starting the first architectural school ever in Russia. Trezzini's surviving structures in St. Petersburg include, in addition to the Summer Palace, the Peter-Paul fortress and its church, the building housing Peter's twelve administrative colleges, and the church of the Annunciation at the Alexander-Nevsky monastery, founded by Peter to shelter the remains of the medieval warrior-saint Alexander of the Neva, who had defeated German forces at a site believed to be nearby (Fig. 34). Trezzini also first laid out the famous Nevsky Prospekt (Avenue), the great long street connecting the Admiralty and the monastery that quickly became the city's main thoroughfare.

Trezzini's best pupil, Mikhail Zemtsov, went on to design buildings for St. Petersburg (for example, the church of Sts. Simeon and Anna, which survives much in its original form) and to train dozens of other native builders who in their turn disseminated the new architecture throughout the Russian Empire. But Jean-Baptiste Alexandre Le Blond, hired by Peter's agents in France in 1716, is generally considered the ablest of the first architects of St. Petersburg, where he worked from August of that year until his sudden death from smallpox in February 1719. Le Blond was particularly accomplished at designing gardens and noble townhouses, both of which he did for St. Petersburg and particularly for suburban Peterhof, the would-be Russian Versailles, whose parks and palaces still retain strong evidence of his influence (Fig. 24). The other architectural creators of St. Petersburg, always working under the close supervision of Peter and his designated officials, include Andreas Schlüter, a sculptor and architect well known for his work in Poland and Prussia (the Berlin *Schloss*) whose decorative touches are still to be seen on the exterior of the

Summer Palace; Schlüter's assistant Johann Friedrich Braunstein, active mostly at Peterhof (Fig. 24); Georg-Johann Mattarnowy, Trezzini's Swiss-German collaborator on the second Winter Palace (second of four on the site, built 1719–1721; the last, still standing, was built by B. F. Rastrelli in 1754–1762) and at the Alexander-Nevsky monastery, as well as the architect, most famously, of the Kunstkamera (Fig. 29); and Niccolò Michetti, recruited in Rome, the designer of a palace for Catherine I in Reval (Fig. 35) who did extensive work at Peterhof. They also include Giovanni Maria Fontana, architect of the Menshikov palace among many other projects first in Moscow and then in St. Petersburg. He was also the translator of the Russian edition of Vignola's handbook, which was, as we saw in Chapter 4, the first work on architecture ever published in Russia, where it remained the single best known book on the subject until the end of the eighteenth century. Working with these and other architects were the hundreds of painters and sculptors recruited in Europe to decorate the palaces of St. Petersburg and its suburbs, the most prominent of whom included Philippe Pillemont, Nicolas Pineau, François Pascal Wassoult, Bartolomeo Tarsia, and Hans Conradt Ossner. It would be difficult to exaggerate the cumulative impact of these many architects and decorators in making St. Petersburg the architectural center and trend-setter of the Russian Empire, a role it indisputably played once the Academy of Fine Arts, also discussed in Chapter 4, was founded within its limits.

Yet St. Petersburg embodied the Petrine revolution in many other ways, too. It rapidly became the most important base in Russia of the new navy and modernized army with their respective offices, hospitals, barracks, parade grounds, shipyards, and schools: the center, in other words, of Peter's military and naval revolutions. Its economic importance was nearly as great. The construction of St. Petersburg entailed the production of bricks, tiles, and glass in wholly unprecedented quantities in Russia—by factors of as much as ten to one—and the manufacture for the first time there of cement (*tsement,* another new word). The ship-yards of the St. Petersburg Admiralty alone (Fig. 24) quickly be-came "the largest industrial complex in eighteenth-century Russia," as a leading economic historian has noted. He also observes that St. Petersburg quickly became Russia's largest port and the most important center of its foreign trade, a trade that in the eighteenth century underwent a fifteen-fold increase. Nor was it simply a matter of quantity, or of St. Petersburg as an exporter of raw mate-rials and supplier of finished goods to its hinterland. With the concentration within and around it of Russia's governing elite, the city became Russia's leading emporium of foreign goods. Stan-dards of consumption were thus set in St. Petersburg and fashions established there, both to be emulated by the nobles and mer-chants of other regions, thereby marking their progressive Euro-peanization.[3] By the middle of the eighteenth century thousands of merchants and craftsmen had established their shops and busi-nesses in the city to cater to this trade, along with more than three thousand drivers of coaches or carriages for hire. St. Petersburg would remain the capital of conspicuous consumption in the Rus-sian Empire, its wealthiest and most fashionable city, "a place in which the cosmopolitan elite of Europe could feel at home and at ease," until the Empire's collapse in 1917.[4]

St. Petersburg was also the principal site of Peter's bureaucratic revolution in Russia and the chief beneficiary of the diplomatic revolution that his victories in battle precipitated in Europe. Start-ing in about 1710 Peter ordered various government functions transferred to the new city from Moscow, Archangel, Voronezh, and elsewhere in his realm, including the newly conquered Baltic towns of Riga and Reval. At the same time, he created new gov-ernment offices in St. Petersburg, chiefly the Senate, the central administrative colleges, and the Holy Synod: the last move made the city, at the stroke of his pen, the headquarters of the Russian Orthodox church, displacing "holy Moscow." Other measures ensured that the governors of the reorganized Russian provinces,

including that of Moscow, should report to officials in St. Petersburg. Furthermore, in Peter's provincial reorganization of 1718–
1720 St. Petersburg became the pilot, based on Swedish models,
for a vastly expanded program of local government, one that concerned itself not just with tax-collecting and basic policing but
also with public health and hygiene, garbage collection, fire pre-
vention, building regulation, street and bridge maintenance, and
supervision of public morals.[5] St. Petersburg was to be the administrative as well as the architectural model for Russia's other cities,
in other words, in addition to its role as the political capital of the
country and the residence of all the new foreign ambassadors
assigned to it. These developments naturally added layers of officials, clerks, workers, and servants to the city's permanent population, which by the 1760s had reached about 150,000 (second in
Russia, still, to Moscow's approximately 250,000).

But it was as the new cultural capital of Russia that St. Petersburg best embodied the Petrine revolution, "cultural" to embrace
not only architecture but also the other visual arts, literature
and the sciences, education, theater, music, and manners. The
first systematic training in architecture, as mentioned above, was
instituted in St. Petersburg. Training in contemporary European
painting and the new graphic arts, only recently established in
Moscow, was soon concentrated there as well, a development that
culminated in the foundation of the St. Petersburg Academy of
Fine Arts. So it was with the St. Petersburg Academy of Sciences,
which after its founding in 1724 rapidly became the institutional
hub for the development of mathematics and the natural sciences
in Russia, displacing in this respect Peter's Naval Academy
(founded in St. Petersburg in 1715). Moreover, the Academy of
Sciences, with its subordinate university and other schools, its
press and graphic arts shop, also served for much of the eighteenth
century as the institutional base for the creators of modern Russian, meaning the language in Russia of modern literature, law,
and philosophy as well as science and the fine arts. Virtually all the

creators of modern Russian literature, most notably Vasily Trediakovsky (1703–1769), Mikhailo Lomonosov (1711–1765), and Alexander Sumarokov (1718–1777), spent much of their careers at the St. Petersburg Academy of Sciences, whose press was far and away the leading publisher of books of secular content in eighteenth-century Russia. The Academy was the home, too, of Russia's first law professors, historians, archaeologists, and ethnographers, several of whom were instrumental in creating the University of Moscow.

Equally critical was St. Petersburg's function, from its founder's time, as the wellspring in Russia of modern European theater, music, dance, and fine manners. The first two blossomed briefly in Moscow in the later seventeenth century, with the arrival of choral part-singing from the Ukraine (where it had developed under Polish Roman Catholic influence) and, from Germany, of court theater, or plays produced on Classical and biblical themes by resident foreigners (mostly missionaries and medics). Both of these cultural experiments soon languished owing to the opposition of prominent elements in the church and to the political turbulence at court following the death of Peter's father, Tsar Aleksei (1676). Once Peter was securely on the throne, however, and once he and any number of his company had experienced theater and music in Europe, both arts were firmly implanted in St. Petersburg, where they eventually prospered under court patronage. Thus was replicated, once again, a pattern that had been common in Europe since the Renaissance.

Various court, school, and public theaters produced mostly translated dramas but also the occasional comedy in the new capital in Peter's time, all staged at first by mostly imported performers for local audiences who were often less than appreciative. But the groundwork was being laid for the later flourishing in St. Petersburg, Moscow, and elsewhere in Russia of theater in the modern sense (scripted performances by professional actors for paying audiences). In music, as Peter first suspended (1700) and

then abolished (1721) the patriarchate, replacing it with the Holy
Synod, his court choir steadily superseded the leading church
singers in the development of choral music in Russia. The Imperial Court Choir, as it was called after 1721, sang both in St. Petersburg's main church and at Peter's public celebrations and court
assemblies, its polyphonic music often composed, whether by
Russian or foreign musicians, specially for the occasion. In the
1730s the choir came firmly under Italian direction, thus inaugu-
rating grand opera in Russia as well as what soon became the
dominant—some would say, the excessive—Italian influence on
Russian church music.

The 1730s also witnessed the birth in St. Petersburg of the
Imperial Court Orchestra and the opening of the first Russian
ballet school, events that were similarly rooted in Petrine initiatives. Peter had promoted the development of European-style
martial music in his reorganized army—trumpets and drums, of
course, but also a small wind orchestra for every division—and
orchestral music with winds, horns, strings, and timpani along
with a clavichord or harpsichord soon became a regular part of
court functions in St. Petersburg. So did minuets and other dancing in contemporary Polish, German, or English style. The first
musicians were Germans or Italians imported by Peter's regime or
by resident foreign ambassadors, as were the instruments, though
Russians soon learned to make and play them as well as the better,
if not the best, foreign masters. Grandees like Prince Menshikov
and Peter's sister, Princess Natalia, maintained their own orches-
tras and choirs, and contemporary European or European-style
music and dance quickly became a mandatory feature of the
St. Petersburg social scene, overshadowing the songs and dances
of the Russian or Baltic folk artists who continued to perform.
The modern period in the history of Russian music and dance,
like that in the history of Russian theater, had definitely begun.[6]

Around 1720 a German diplomat living in St. Petersburg observed a "spreading reformation of manners" there, one indication

of the city's budding role as the social center of elite Russia.[7] Another is an etiquette manual entitled *The Honorable Mirror of Youth, or A Guide to Social Conduct Gathered from Various Authors,* which was first published in St. Petersburg in 1717 and reprinted three times during Peter's reign (for a total of nearly 2,000 copies sold) as well as several times thereafter. As both its title and contents show, the manual was compiled from various European sources translated into Russian and was published for the guidance of young Russians aspiring to be "true nobles" and "true courtiers." It contains a long list of rules that proscribe gossiping, lying, drunkenness, gluttony, lechery, boasting, disparaging others, tomfoolery, and "other such crude conduct" while offering advice on how to behave with proper dignity before parents, clergy, servants, and the monarch. "The young nobleman should complete his education especially in languages, horsemanship, dancing, and swordsmanship, and be able to converse well, and in eloquence and book learning to comport himself with such ease as to be a true courtier"; "A truly honorable cavalier must be modest, affable, courteous," must scorn "excess luxury" and live within his means, and must "keep his word"; while the "crown of maidenly honor" was said to consist of some twenty virtues, namely "an inclination for, and love of, God's word and divine service, true knowledge of God, fear of God, appealing to God, gratitude, confessing the faith, deference to parents, industriousness, decency, affability, charity, bodily cleanliness, modesty, abstinence, chastity, thrift, generosity, truthfulness, and reserve."

We cannot, of course, know to what extent the standards of gentlemanly and maidenly behavior laid down in this manual ever took hold among the Russian elite—although readers of Russian literature of the late eighteenth and early nineteenth centuries will recognize in various characters their fictional embodiments. Elite memoirs of the period similarly suggest successful efforts to assimilate the new manners.[8] There is also some anecdotal evidence, mainly in the comments of contemporary European visitors like the German diplomat quoted above, that while progress in this respect was at first slow, fitful, or merely superficial, it was remarkable nonetheless. And we might note that in his *Discourse* first published in St. Petersburg in 1717 defending the Russian cause in the Northern War, Peter Shafirov at one point remarks on how "we now see . . . several thousand of His [Peter's] subjects of the Russian nation, male and female, skilled in various European languages . . . and of such conduct moreover that they can be compared without shame to all other European peoples." It was, no doubt about it, a solid start. The customary servility and rustic coarseness of traditional Russian manners along with Muscovite isolationism were being supplanted among the elite by the cosmopolitan courtesies of the European upper classes.[9]

In such many and varied ways—military, naval, commercial-industrial, governmental, diplomatic, cultural—did St. Petersburg embody the revolution of Peter the Great. Still, it would be wrong to represent its development from military outpost to cosmopolitan European city as some sort of uninterrupted triumphal progress, which surviving visual depictions—stylized prints, drawings, and paintings—might seem to suggest. The successive verbal accounts of discriminating European visitors offer more revealing impressions of St. Petersburg's early years, and we might therefore sample some of them.[10]

A special report to his government from the first regular British ambassador to Russia, Charles Whitworth, affords a chilly glimpse of St. Petersburg in 1710:

> The foundations of this new town were laid in hopes it might one day prove a second Amsterdam or Venice. To people it the nobility have been ordered to remove hither from the farthest parts of the country, though with no small difficulty, since the climate is too cold and the ground too marshy to furnish the conveniences of life, which are all brought from the neighbouring countries. However the Tsar

is charmed with his new production and would lose the best of his provinces sooner than this barren corner. The fortress is built on a separate island, with good stone bastions laid on piles, but of much too narrow an extent to make any considerable defense in case of attack. The floods in autumn are very inconvenient, sometimes rising in the night to the first floors, so that the cattle are often swept away and the inhabitants scarce saved by their upper story . . . The river is seldom or never clear of ice before the middle of May, and the ships cannot hold [back from] the sea any longer than the end of September without great danger.

F. C. Weber, the resident German diplomat quoted earlier, left a description of the city as it was in 1720 that similarly describes the severity of its climate, the periodic flooding, the coerced character of its residential development, the poverty of the surrounding countryside, the high cost of living there (everything imported, from abroad or from the Russian interior), the shortcomings of the methods and materials employed in building, and the mass of poor, one-room wooden huts that made up the bulk as yet of the city's ordinary housing. But Weber also praised the regulations introduced by Peter for extinguishing fires and "for keeping his new city in good order, the great encouragements given to architects, mechanics, and all other imaginable sorts of artificers," and "the improvements which the Tsar has made not merely calculated for profit, but for delight also." Thus:

> He has built splendid pleasure houses, raised noble gardens and adorned them with greenhouses, aviaries and menageries, grottos, cascades, and all other sorts of water-works. He has placed in the steeple of the fortress a chime made in Holland. He has ordered assemblies to be kept in the winter; operas, plays, and concerts of music are to be set up for the diversion of his court; and in order to engage foreigners to frequent it,

drafts [architectural plans] have already been made and proper places marked out to build houses for those purposes.

Weber once heard Prince Menshikov boast that some day St. Petersburg would be "another Venice, to which foreigners would travel thither purely out of curiosity." Reflecting on his nearly six years of living in the city and watching it grow—from "a heap of villages linked together" to "a wonder of the world, considering its magnificent palaces, thousands of houses, and the short time employed in the building of it"—Weber did not think Menshikov's boast was an idle one.

Nor did Friedrich Wilhelm von Bergholtz, a German nobleman who had spent much of his youth in Russia (his father was a general in Peter's army) and later returned as a companion to the duke of Holstein, who was courting Peter's daughter, Anna. Bergholtz kept a detailed diary from his arrival in St. Petersburg in June 1721, when he found the city "changed so much since I left [in 1717] that I scarcely recognized it," to the end of 1725, by which time the duke had won his suit and the couple had left for home. His diary's generally positive descriptions of the rediscovered city begin with the Nevsky Prospekt, "a long, wide avenue paved in stone" that had been built in the last few years: "Notwithstanding that the three or four rows of trees on either side of it are still not large, it is extraordinarily beautiful by reason of its enormous extent and state of cleanliness . . . It makes a more wonderful sight than any I have ever beheld anywhere." The Admiralty was "a huge and beautiful building," the park adjacent to the Summer Palace contained "everything that could be wanted in a pleasure garden," while the church in the Peter-Paul fortress was the "largest and most beautiful" in St. Petersburg. "Above it," Bergholtz continues,

rises a high steeple in the new style, covered in brightly gilded copper plates which look extraordinarily fine in the sunlight. The chimes in its steeple are as large and fine as those at the Admiralty . . . This fine church is entirely of masonry construction, and not in the Byzantine but in the new taste, adorned with prominent arches and columns and, front and side, a splendid portico.

From the steeple of the Peter-Paul church at noon one day in August 1721, Bergholtz and his master viewed the city spread out below them:

Petersburg has the shape of an oval and is of enormous extent. In many places it is still meagerly built, but these gaps will not be slow to fill up if the Tsar lives longer. The fortress has several thick and high masonry bastions fitted with a large number of cannon. They say that its rapid construction cost countless lives.

In this last remark Bergholtz cautiously invoked the allegation, repeated in other foreigners' accounts and acquiring thereafter the force of legend, that in its early years tens of thousands of workers—"60,000" in seven years, "100,000" in eight, "300,000" in its first decade or so—had lost their lives in the construction of St. Petersburg (note again that the city's total population in 1725 was 40,000, and that between 1703 and 1725 somewhere between 10,000 and 30,000 construction workers, conscripted in two-month shifts, labored annually in the city).[11] Which is not to deny that in these same years the death toll among workers seems to have been unusually high for the time owing to the severity of the climate, rampant sickness, and the shortage of provisions, a situation not unknown elsewhere in the world when large-scale building projects have been undertaken in harsh and unfamiliar terrain and before mostly twentieth-century medical advances in the control of malaria—"swamp fever"—and other such infectious diseases were available. In the case of St. Petersburg, steps were

promptly taken to improve conditions at the worksite, including—another first for Russia—such rudimentary medical measures as were known at the time.

Bergholtz also recorded his impressions of the suburban palace-
estates that were in various stages of construction in the early
1720s and especially of Peterhof, whose buildings and grounds
were nearer completion than the others (Fig. 36). There Peter's
favorite residence, Monplaisir, was in Bergholtz's view "a small but
very nice house, decorated most notably with many choice Dutch
paintings." The main palace on its hill comprised two stories, the
lower containing

> large and fine hallways with pretty columns; and above there
> is a splendid hall whence one has a wonderful view of the sea
> and, in the distance, of Petersburg . . . The rooms in general
> are small but not bad, and are hung with fine paintings and
> provided with beautiful furniture. Especially remarkable is
> the cabinet [study] containing a small library belonging to
> the Tsar made up of various Dutch and Russian books; it was
> done by a French craftsman [Nicolas Pineau] and is distin-
> guished by its excellent carved decoration.

The large garden behind the main palace was "very beautifully
laid out," while before it Bergholtz discovered a "magnificent
cascade, as wide as the palace itself, made of natural stone and decorated with gilded lead figures in relief against a green background." A fine canal connected the cascade to the Finnish Gulf,
where a small harbor had been built, thus permitting access to
Peterhof by boat, "which is very agreeable and convenient."
Finally, the Lower Park, spread out beneath the main palace on
either side of the cascade and canal, was

> intersected by many fine and pleasant alleys shaded by groves
> of trees. The two principal alleys lead from the two sides of

the Park through a grove of trees to two pleasure houses located exactly the same distance from the palace and the Gulf. To the right is Monplaisir, in whose garden, also surrounded by trees, grow many beautiful bushes, plants, and flowers; here there are also a large pond with swans and other fowl swimming in it, a little house for them, and various other structures built for fun. At the opposite end of the alley from Monplaisir a similar garden and house [to be called Marly], already begun, will be completed.

The buildings and grounds of Peterhof, designed and built by Le Blond, Braunstein, and various other masters and workers and completed in stages in the eighteenth century, were largely destroyed during World War II. They have since been restored to something like their original condition and are now among the most popular sights of greater St. Petersburg. Strolling around Peterhof, enjoying its views of the gulf while traversing its gardens and rooms, one can feel the strength of Peter's personal attachment to Europe and, still more, to the sea.

The largely positive accounts of St. Petersburg and its suburban palaces left by European visitors in Peter's last years contrast notably with their largely negative accounts of Moscow at roughly the same time. Indeed, these contrasting accounts provide some of the best evidence available that during the course of Peter's reign an architectural revolution had taken place. But in the years just after Peter's death European visitors to St. Petersburg recorded more mixed impressions of the new city. Pierre Deschisaux, for example, a French physician and botanist in search of a job (which he did not find), deplored the Summer Garden—"divided up, in the Dutch manner, into various compartments, bowers, arbors of one sort or another, fenced enclosures, and other such bits and pieces as are called vulgarly *le colifichets* [gewgaws]"—while praising the Admiralty ensemble for the "good order with which its canals, yards, storerooms, lodgings, roperies, and other parts" were laid out. Deschisaux was appalled by the flood he experienced in November 1726, when the various tributaries of the Neva "joined together to form one great sea, on the surface of which the city seemed to float." He had to take refuge for several days in the attic of his house. Worse was to come. The death in 1727 of Peter's wife and successor, Empress Catherine I, and the accession of his twelve-year-old grandson, Peter II (son of Tsarevich Aleksei), precipitated a palace revolution that saw the banishment of Menshikov and the return of the court to Moscow. St. Petersburg assumed the appearance of a ghost town. Such is the picture conveyed in the letters to a friend back in England of Mrs. Thomas Ward (later Lady Rondeau), wife of the newly appointed British consul-general, not long after arriving in 1729. St. Petersburg, she observed, was "pleasantly situated" on its river and several islands (she arrived in June), the church in the fortress was "fine," but though the "houses and streets" of the merchants' quarter were "very handsome, they are uninhabited." Similarly, "there are many fine houses in the town belonging to the nobility, but now, in the absence of the court, quite empty." Her visit to Peterhof produced the same reaction. She noticed, for instance, that while "some good pictures" were hanging in the main palace they were "much spoiled for want of care." And with that she left for Moscow.

Empress Anna (1730–1740), Peter's niece, whom he had married to the duke of Courland (on the Baltic), where she had lived for twenty years, brought the court back to St. Petersburg, this time for good. The city resumed its rapid growth, though now in a largely uncontrolled fashion, and in 1736–1737 it suffered extensive damage from fire. A master plan for St. Petersburg's continued development was drawn up, ensuring its future as the Russian Empire's capital (Fig. 32). And it was about then, in the summer of 1739, that another visitor, Count Francesco Algarotti, arrived.

Algarotti, a scientist and *littérateur*, was well connected in European high society, and his letters from St. Petersburg circulated widely in Italian, French, German, and English printed editions.

His comments on what he saw were predictably sharp—both witty and severe. Entering the Neva estuary he was ostensibly shocked to find that the river, "this sacred way," was "not adorned with either arches or temples" but rather was "flanked by forest to both left and right—and that not of majestic oaks or tufted elms or evergreen laurels, but of the most wretched species of trees on which the sun shines." His first glimpse of St. Petersburg seemed to make up for its dreary approaches, for

> all of a sudden the river bends; the scene instantly changes, as in an opera, and we behold before us the Imperial city. On either bank groups of sumptuous edifices, towers topped by gilded spires, ships with banners flying . . . such is the brilliant spectacle that greets us. Here, they tell us, is the Admiralty, there the Arsenal; here the fortress, there the Academy; ahead, the Winter Palace.

When Algarotti and his party actually set foot in the city, however, their view changed yet again: "we no longer found it as superb as it appeared from a distance, perhaps because the gloominess of the forest no longer brightened our perspective." On the one hand, "the situation of a city located on the banks of a large river and made up of various islands, providing different vantage points and optical effects, could only be beautiful"; on the other, "the ground on which it is founded is low and marshy, the materials of which it is constructed are of little value, and the designs of the buildings are not by an Inigo Jones or a Palladio [the famous English and Italian architects]." Indeed, "there reigns in this capital a kind of bastard architecture, one which partakes of the Italian, the French, and the Dutch." The suburban villas of the grandees fared no better in this critic's eyes, as "one sees clearly that they were built more in obedience than by choice. Their walls are all cracked, out of plumb, and remain standing with difficulty." This provoked the witticism that "elsewhere ruins make themselves, while in St. Petersburg they are built."[12]

Algarotti's most memorable remark, however, applied to the metropolis as a whole, which he had come to see, he said, purely out of curiosity, to discover for himself "this new city" created by Peter, "this great window recently opened in the north through which Russia looks on Europe." The metaphor would long outlive its author. Pushkin would describe St. Petersburg as Russia's window on Europe in his great poem about Peter and his city, "The Bronze Horseman" (1833); and countless other commentators have recalled it, often distorted to "window on the West," ever since. Yet effective as it might at first seem, the metaphor is too passive. For St. Petersburg was from the outset a great doorway as well, one through which countless Europeans, bearing their values and their ways, poured into Russia, there to help implement, in one way or another, the Petrine revolution.

Indeed, the city had survived, and more than just survived, both the death of its founder and the return of the monarch to Moscow. It was soon to enter, in the reign of Empress Elizabeth, Peter's daughter, another great building boom, rendering it, in the eyes of a well-traveled British merchant, "an elegant and superb city."[13] A virtually continuous process of development—architectural, governmental, naval, commercial, industrial, and demographic—ensued, and by the early nineteenth century St. Petersburg was the most populous as well as the most important city of the Russian Empire, an "imperial colossus" from which more than one-sixth of the land surface of the earth was ultimately ruled.[14] In 1914, on the outbreak of war with Germany, its long-standing Germanic name was officially russified to Petrograd, "Peter's city" by another name. A few years later, in 1917, it became the crucible of the revolutions that toppled the monarchy and propelled the Bolsheviks under Lenin into power. Fearing for its own survival in the face of what looked like an imminent German invasion (World War I was still waging), the Bolshevik government, early in 1918, moved Russia's capital back to Moscow, which became the capital under Stalin of the Soviet Union. On Lenin's death, in 1924, the city was renamed Leningrad in a transparent attempt to replace the aura of Peter and all it stood for with that of Lenin. It was not to last. The city survived Soviet rule, or misrule, as well as the horrific German siege of World War II by a mixture of pride and courage, wit and perseverance, a spirit best captured, perhaps, in the person and poetry of Anna Akhmatova (1889–1966), whose complex masterpiece, *Poem without a Hero,* evokes the city's magnificent literary tradition from Pushkin to herself. "A different time is drawing near," she wrote in 1919, prophetically, "The wind of death already chills the heart; / But the holy city of Peter / Will be our unintended monument."[15] In 1991, following the collapse of the Soviet Union, its citizens voted to restore the city's original name. And as St. Petersburg, again, it would celebrate its tercentenary in 2003, a monument, now, to the courage of Akhmatova and her generation as well as to Peter and his revolution.

Conclusion

Since this is an interpretive history of the reign of Peter the Great rather than a simple biography, it may be helpful to recapitulate its core argument. That argument, I would stress, is historical in nature, meaning that it is based primarily on my studies over the past thirty years and more of written documents from Peter's time and of the material remains of his reign to be found in St. Petersburg, Moscow, and elsewhere in Russia. It also draws on my reading of a large volume of work by historians and other scholars—archaeologists, literary, language, music, and art specialists—published in Russian, English, and other languages since the eighteenth century. I emphasize this background because, like any serious work of history, this book is not just a collation of the author's opinions based mainly on his personal philosophy and life experiences and artfully designed to provoke or please. Such collations, it seems, are increasingly being offered to the public in the guise of real history. On the other hand, this book is deliberately concise: the contemporary written and material or visual sources on which it is primarily based are only occasionally quoted or reproduced for the reader to see for herself. Nor are the many scholarly works consulted more than occasionally cited in the chapter notes. For the most part, then, the reader must take it on faith that the depiction and analysis of persons and events and the overall interpretation of Peter's reign that are tendered here are solidly grounded in the relevant sources and scholarship. English editions of two of those sources as well as a selection of the best of that scholarship are listed in the Further Reading section.

The argument unfolded in this book is simple to state in summary form. The roughly thirty-year reign of Peter I in Russia witnessed a number of major developments, each more or less revolutionary in its Russian context, which together produced what can fairly be called a cultural revolution. The term was defined early in Chapter 4 to mean changes in culture that were major and seen as such at the time, that happened relatively suddenly, that were consciously intended, and that produced transformations which were lasting. As judged by these criteria, the manifold changes in building, visualizing, and verbalizing that were introduced in Russia under Peter in connection with his many reforms were such as to constitute a cultural revolution. The essence of that revolution was a rapid and sweeping Europeanization of Russian ways of making and doing things, and of thinking and talking about them. And Europeanization, in that day and age, was equivalent to modernization.

History is about context—not just about people and events, but about people and events in their immediate settings. Chapters 2 and 3 were devoted to contextualizing the military, naval, diplomatic, and bureaucratic initiatives undertaken by Peter's regime to meet the challenges the country faced or to fulfill the ambitions of its leader. War was the engine of profound changes in government and society everywhere in early modern Europe, and war with a militarily more advanced Sweden was the main external factor propelling the Petrine revolution. True, war against the Crimean vassals of the Ottoman Empire—the Azov campaigns of 1695 and 1696, the first a failure, the second victorious—impelled a modest modernization of Peter's armed forces, especially with respect to siegecraft and joint military-naval operations. But it was the long and initially disastrous war against Sweden that engendered a wholesale modernization of Russia's army—bringing it up to contemporary European standards in tactics and strategy, discipline and training, equipment and supply—as well as the creation of a navy comparable to those deployed by the kings of Denmark and Sweden, the longtime contenders for supremacy in the Baltic region. Such a drastic program entailed the introduction of annual troop levies (conscription), the imposition of new taxes (culminating in the universal "soul tax"), the development of industry, the building of modern warships and new-style fortifications, the recruitment of vastly more foreign experts than had ever before worked in Russia, and the learning by Russians of countless new foreign words and ways (foreign usually meant German, a matter of geographical proximity; but with regard to the navy, as we have seen, it usually meant Dutch, Italian, or English). Peter's program also entailed a wholesale reform of the state, essentially through the creation of a new-style bureaucracy capable of financing and directing the new navy and modernized army. All these more or less radical changes in support of Russia's greatly augmented armed forces naturally had their impact on society and the economy, newly regimenting the elite and further burdening the masses while significantly expanding both industry and foreign trade.[1]

Victory in the Northern War established the newly named Russian Empire as the leading power in northeastern Europe, which occasioned in turn a diplomatic revolution in the European state system. Thereafter no major question that divided the European powers except the partition of Africa was settled without Russian participation, which as often as not was decisive. Russian ambassadors took up residence in all the European capitals, and Russian rulers and their designated heirs married into European, usually German, royal families (German not only because of the links established by Peter I but also because of the plethora of German royal houses). The Russian official-noble elite now spoke German,

French, and/or English as well as their native tongue and frequently also intermarried with their European counterparts (or their non-Russian counterparts within the Russian Empire). In fact, the Imperial Russian elite became a remarkably cosmopolitan class, at home in the capitals and resorts of Europe nearly as much as they were in St. Petersburg or Moscow or on their country estates.

But the prolonged, eventually successful prosecution of the Northern War was certainly not the only factor impelling the Petrine revolution in Russia, even in its military and political aspects. Peter's own character, tastes, and interests along with those of leading members of his company (like Menshikov or Prokopovich) were also a major factor. So, to a lesser extent, were the material and career concerns of numerous other members of the Petrine elite—the "several thousand subjects of the Russian nation, male and female," in the words of one of them (Peter Shafirov), who had become "skilled in various European languages . . . and of such conduct moreover that they can be compared without shame to all other European peoples" (Chap. 6). These several thousand individuals, many of them (like Shafirov) foreign in origin, had gone to school on Peter's orders, had served in his army and navy, had entered his bureaucracy or his diplomatic service, had adopted the new dress and manners at his behest, and had built and furnished their homes in the new style. In short, they had invested their futures and those of their children in the new Russia. We must not underestimate the complex of personal motives and passions driving and sustaining the Petrine revolution, a point frequently made, if only in passing, throughout this book and particularly in Chapter 1.

The personal factor was especially important in fueling the revolution in Russian culture that occurred in Peter's time. This was the subject of Chapter 4, in many ways the heart of the book. There, the innumerable cultural tracks or traces of Peter's many reforms were discussed under the general headings of architecture, imagery, and language or, better, verbal culture: verbal as distinct from the more purely visual arts of architecture and imagery, and verbal as the core of any human culture worthy of the name. Drawing on the material presented in Chapters 2 and 3, it was argued that each of Peter's grand revolutionary projects—his creation of the navy, massive reorganization of the army, bureaucratization of the state, and injection of Russia into Europe, all justified by the invention of a new theory of monarchy—entailed the adoption by Russians of countless new cultural ways. The result was an architectural revolution that laid the foundations in Russia of a modern built environment, a revolution in imagery and image-making that brought Russia into the mainstream of modern visual art, and a revolution in linguistic practices, values, and norms that proved to be the crucial first stage in the constitution of a modern verbal culture in Russia, one that necessarily included a standardized literary language (modern Russian). All of this is documented at length in the relevant scholarly works listed among the Further Reading suggestions. More difficult to prove is the advent in Russia in conjunction with the Petrine revolution of a typically modern mentality, one that could be characterized as scientific in outlook or, more broadly, secular. As indicated at various points in this book, evidence of such a mental revolution occurring among a small portion of the Petrine elite, including Peter himself, does seem to exist (Peter's dream-records, for instance; Prokopovich's political theory; their jointly designed church reform; the foundation of the St. Petersburg Academy of Sciences). Such evidence is certainly available in ever-growing abundance in the succeeding history of Russia, whose scientists, thinkers, writers, and artists contributed greatly not just to the promotion of modernity in Russia itself but to the creation and maintenance of a modern world culture, one that through mass education and the mass media has spread across the globe.

One test of modernity, most people would agree, is how a given society treats its women. Patriarchalism—the subordination of women to men in religion, law, government, the family—has been a well-nigh universal feature of human history, as it certainly was of Muscovite society; and the question naturally arises, What impact did the Petrine revolution have in this respect? Readers will have noticed that Peter's sister Natalia seems to have enjoyed greater freedom of movement than did their mother, bound up as she was in reclusive Muscovite traditions that her daughter had largely abandoned for the new European ways (Chap. 1). Peter's new succession law (Chap. 3) opened the way for women fully and formally to rule in Russia, as they did for the next sixty-six of the seventy-five years following his death, beginning with his wife Catherine I (his law was repealed, by the misogynist Emperor Paul, in 1797). Women were explicitly enjoined by Peter, even required, to forsake their customary seclusion and to join their menfolk at the social gatherings or "assemblies" that he organized on the courtly European model, there to be dressed in the freer, finer, more becoming "German" style. Mixed company thus became the norm in Russian high society, if at first only in St. Petersburg.

Elite Russian women were also encouraged by Peter to learn European languages and to adopt European manners (Chap. 6), the better to represent official Russia both at home and abroad. Prearranged or forced marriages were outlawed by him, rape was severely punished in his Military and Naval Statutes, and provision was made for illegitimate children to be delivered anonymously to orphanages without penalty to the mother. Still more, the property rights of elite women were strengthened; and with enactment of the Table of Ranks, whereby a wife automatically acquired the status of her husband, women of the lower orders could rise in society with their men. In these and other ways Peter broke with Muscovite conventions and traditions, usually sanctioned by the church, and improved the status of female members of the official-noble elite in conformity with contemporary European norms.[2] It was a definite step forward for Russia, and a compelling model for subsequent rulers and elites to emulate. But the case of women also provides a telling example of the initially quite limited social impact of the Petrine revolution. Some improvement in their legal status, new opportunities for upward social mobility, and greater freedom of movement in high society did not signal a drastic change of condition for elite Russian women by comparison with their men. Nor did these advances have any bearing whatever on the lives of the vast majority of more ordinary Russian women.

Indeed, the often radically new values and behavioral norms directly or indirectly imposed on society by the Petrine revolution provoked, as we have seen (Chap. 5), widespread resistance—and not only among peasants and ordinary townsfolk but also, in varying degrees, among the merchants, lower clergy, and provincial nobility. These groups, along with elements of the popular masses, were only gradually incorporated in the new Russia through education, through promotion in government service, the armed forces, or the church, and eventually through urbanization, industrialization, and the mass media. A widening socioeconomic and related cultural gap has attended the earlier stages of modernization in most parts of the world, and Russia was no exception. In Russia as recently as the beginning of the twentieth century the gap between Europeanized elite and peasant-worker masses, though rapidly closing, was still wide, a function of both the sheer size of the country and the persistent rurality of much of its economy. Yet it would be quite wrong—unhistorical—to blame Peter the Great for Russia's condition some two hundred years after his death, as if he were responsible not only for his own shortcomings but for those of his successors, particularly the folly of emancipating the nobility from compulsory state service (1762) without emancipating their peasants from their control (not until 1861).

The revolution of Peter the Great was not mainly social or economic in character, as we have seen, though its impact in both spheres was considerable. It was, rather, a political and, still more, a cultural revolution of wide-ranging consequences. And the essence of that revolution, it deserves emphasis, was Europeanization or, in its eighteenth-century context, modernization. As Russia under Peter became part of the European state system, thanks to his military victories and related diplomatic efforts, its government and elite culture underwent rapid and intensive Europeanization. The outcome by the end of the century was a major European power—one that would soon play a decisive role in the Napoleonic wars (1796–1815)—and an elite culture poised to enter its Golden Age, an age personified by the poet Alexander Pushkin (1799–1837). We cannot fairly credit Peter with the subsequent political and cultural achievements of Imperial Russia, no more than we can fairly blame him for its subsequent social and economic deficiencies. We can, however, trace both sets of consequences, one way or another, to the revolution he led.

A further point must be made. The necessary emphasis in this book on Europe and on Europeanization in Russia should not be construed to negate the Asian dimension of Russian history and, indeed, geography. From the earliest times Russians have expanded eastward as well as to the north, south, and west; eastern peoples and cultures—Mongol-Tatar, Turkish, Persian, and other— have had their impact on Russia, too. By the end of the nineteenth century virtually all of northern Asia lay within Russian borders. But in demographic, economic, or almost any other terms—certainly cultural—the western or European parts of Russia have weighed far more heavily in the historical balance than have the Asian. And it was the Petrine revolution that decisively tipped the balance in Europe's direction.

St. Petersburg remains the great monument to Peter's revolution in Russia. The straight streets, broad avenues, and intersecting canals of the central city, its oldest parks and buildings, its Peter-Paul fortress and church, its celebrated statue of the Bronze Horseman, are all potent reminders of the city's founder. This is particularly true of St. Petersburg's very location, on the Baltic Sea at the extreme western edge of the Russian heartland. Its choice as the site of Russia's capital, which it remained for two hundred years, is explicable only in terms of Peter's vision of making Russia an integral part of Europe—of bringing Russia into the modern world. We may hope that with the restoration of St. Petersburg's original name after some seventy years of Soviet rule, its founder's vision will also be fully restored.

Chronology
Notes
Further Reading
Index

Chronology

All dates are given according to the Julian or Old Style calendar used in Russia, by decree of Peter, from January 1, 1700. In the eighteenth century this calendar was eleven days behind the now universal Gregorian or New Style calendar that was gradually superseding it in Europe (to be adopted in Russia in 1918).

1598–1613	"Time of Troubles" in Russia, ending in accession of first ruler of the Romanov dynasty, Tsar Michael
1645–1676	Reign of Tsar Aleksei, son of Tsar Michael, father of Peter I
1649	Promulgation of the *Ulozhenie* (law code), formal enserfment of Russian peasantry
1660s	Church schism, emergence of Old Believer and other sects
1667	Peace of Andrusovo with Poland, ceding eastern Ukraine with Kiev to Russia; confirmed by treaty of 1686
1670–1671	Razin rebellion
1672	Birth of Peter I "the Great" (May 30)
1676–1682	Reign of Tsar Feodor III, elder half-brother of Peter
1682	Accession of Peter I and Ivan V, younger half-brother of Peter, as co-tsars (April)

1682–1689	Regency of Sophia, sister of Ivan, half-sister of Peter
1689	Marriage of Peter and Evdokia Lopukhina (January)
1689	Sophia deposed, beginning of Peter's personal reign (September)
1693, 1694	Peter sails on the White Sea and Arctic Ocean (summers)
1694	Death of Tsaritsa Natalia, mother of Peter (January 25)
1695, 1696	Russian campaigns against Azov (summers)
1696	Death of Ivan V (January 29); Peter now sole tsar in name as well as in fact
1696	Preobrazhensky Office given jurisdiction over political offenses
1696	Foundation of the Admiralty
1697–1698	Peter's Grand Embassy to Europe
1698	*Streltsy* revolt in Moscow
1700	Adoption of European (Julian) calendar in Russia (January 1)
1700	Death of Patriarch Adrian, suspension of the patriarchate (abolished 1721)
1700	Russian defeat at Narva (November)
1701	Creation of the Moscow School of Mathematics and Navigation
1702	Russian conquest of Nöteborg
1703	Publication of the Moscow *Gazette (Vedomosti)*, Russia's first newspaper
1703	Foundation of St. Petersburg (May 16)
1705–1706	Astrakhan uprising
1707–1708	Bulavin rebellion
1708–1710	Creation of the Russian "civil" alphabet
1708	Hetman Mazepa of Ukraine renounces allegiance to Peter, joins Swedish invaders
1709	Russian victory at Poltava in eastern Ukraine (June 27)

1711	Foundation of the Senate (March)
1711	Russian defeat by Turks at the Pruth in Moldavia (July)
1711	Marriage of Tsarevich Aleksei and Princess Charlotte of Wolfenbüttel (October)
1712	Marriage of Peter and Catherine
1714	Russian naval victory off Hangö Head
1715	Creation of the St. Petersburg Naval Academy
1716	Promulgation of the *Military Statute*
1716	Death of Tsarevna Natalia, Peter's sister (born 1673)
1716–1717	Peter's second tour of Europe
1718	Trial and death of Tsarevich Aleksei (born 1690)
1718–1720	Establishment of the administrative colleges—of War, Foreign Affairs, Justice, etc.—in St. Petersburg; provincial government reform
1720	Promulgation of the *Naval Statute* and the *General Regulation*
1721	Promulgation of the *Ecclesiastical Regulation,* creation of the Holy Synod
1721	Peace of Nystad (August 30)
1721	Peter proclaimed Emperor (October 22)
1722	Promulgation of the Table of Ranks and law on the succession to the throne
1722–1723	Russian war with Persia
1722–1724	Completion of the first universal (male) census; first collection of the soul tax (abolished 1887)
1724	Foundation of the St. Petersburg Academy of Sciences
1724	Coronation of Catherine as Empress (May 7)
1725	Death of Peter (January 28)
1725–1727	Reign of Catherine I
1727–1730	Reign of Peter II, grandson of Peter
1729	Death of Alexander Menshikov (born 1673)
1730–1740	Reign of Anna, niece of Peter
1736	Death of Feofan Prokopovich (born 1682)

1741–1761	Reign of Elizabeth, daughter of Peter
1745	Publication of the *Atlas Russica*
1757	Foundation of the St. Petersburg Academy of Fine Arts
1761–1762	Reign of Peter III, grandson of Peter (December–June)
1762	Emancipation of the nobility from compulsory state service (February)
1762–1796	Reign of Catherine II, wife of Peter III
1773–1775	Pugachev rebellion
1796–1801	Reign of Paul, son of Catherine II; restoration (1797) of succession to throne by male primogeniture
1861	Proclamation of serf emancipation
1917	Collapse of monarchy (February–March), Bolshevik Revolution (October)

Notes

The full titles of all references cited here in short form only can be found in the Further Reading list at the end of the book.

1. Peter and Company

1. A detailed account of these events is in Hughes, *Sophia*, pp. 52–88.

2. The "German Settlement" was the preserve, outside Moscow, of resident European merchants and their dependents and of the numerous European soldiers, artists, and technical experts in Russian service. The majority of these residents were from Germany, Britain, and Holland; hence the Settlement itself, with its Roman Catholic and Protestant churches, its taverns, houses and gardens, formed a western European island in the surrounding Russian sea.

3. *Pis'ma i bumagi imperatora Petra Velikogo*, 13 vols. to date (St. Petersburg, 1887–), 4, no. 1179 (p. 184). This huge, still incomplete collection of Peter's letters and papers is hereafter cited *PiB*, followed by volume, item, and page numbers.

4. N. I. Pavlenko, *Aleksandr Danilovich Menshikov*, 3rd ed. (Moscow, 1989).

5. Thomas Consett, *The Present State and Regulations of the Church of Russia . . . [with a Preface] wherein is contained a full and genuine Account of the Rise and Fall of Prince Menshikoff* (London, 1729), p. xlvii.

6. *Tryal of the Czarewitz Alexis Petrowitz* ... (London, 1718), p. 10. This is a contemporary English translation of the official account of Aleksei's trial, which was published in Russian in St. Petersburg in 1718, as well as in French and German editions—making the "Aleksei affair" an event, or scandal, of European proportions.

7. Bushkovitch, *Peter the Great*, chaps. 9, 10.

8. Quoted in Cracraft, *Church Reform*, p. 10.

9. *PiB*, 1, no. 37 (p. 28).

10. *PiB*, 1, no. 40 (pp. 31-32).

11. Prince Boris Kurakin, "Gistoriia o tsare Petre," in M. I. Semevsky, ed., *Arkhiv Kn. F. A. Kurakina*, 1 (St. Petersburg, 1890), pp. 71-74.

12. Friedrich Christian Weber, *The Present State of Russia*, authorized English translation from the original German, vol. 1 (London, 1723), pp. 89-90.

13. Reports of the French ambassador, Campredon, as cited in Cracraft, *Church Reform*, p. 13.

14. Weber, *The Present State of Russia*, pp. 90-91.

15. V. O. Kliuchevsky, *Sochineniia*, 4 (Moscow, 1958), p. 41.

16. So argues Ernest Zitser, in a fascinating study entitled *The Transfigured Kingdom: Politics and Charismatic Authority at the Court of Peter the Great* (Ithaca, N.Y., forthcoming).

17. See further James Cracraft, "Some Dreams of Peter the Great," *Canadian-American Slavic Studies* 8, no. 2, pp. 173-197; reprinted, without the source notes, in Cracraft, ed., *Peter Transforms Russia*, pp. 231-258.

18. A large sample of this portraiture is reproduced in Cracraft, *Revolution in Imagery*, passim; see especially figures 21, 61-63, 65, 69, 71, 72.

19. Riasanovsky, *Image of Peter*, is a detailed discussion of this question.

20. See Cracraft, *Church Reform*.

21. Anisimov, *Reforms of Peter*, p. 267.

22. See [Jacob von] Staehlin, *Original Anecdotes of Peter the Great* (London, 1788), no. 110 (pp. 355-363); Staehlin, an early member of the St. Petersburg Academy of Sciences founded by Peter, was told the story by Peter's doctors.

23. Described in Richard S. Wortman, *Scenarios of Power: Myth and Ceremony in Russian Monarchy*, 1 (Princeton, 1995), pp. 75-78.

24. Harold B. Segel, ed. and trans., *The Literature of Eighteenth-Century Russia*, 1 (New York, 1967), p. 141, followed by a translation of the oration (pp. 142–148).

25. Hughes, *Age of Peter*, p. 262.

2. Military and Naval Revolutions

1. Geoffrey Parker, *The Military Revolution: Military Innovation and the Rise of the West* (Cambridge, England, 1988), is a good introduction to this subject.

2. Figures from Frank Tallett, *War and Society in Early Modern Europe, 1495–1715* (New York, 1992), p. 13, and Euan Cameron, ed., *Early Modern Europe* (Oxford, England, 1999), p. 307.

3. R. M. Hatton, *Charles XII of Sweden* (New York, 1968), remains the best study of Charles in English.

4. The main works in English on Russian military history are J. L. H. Keep, *Soldiers of the Tsar: Army and Society in Russia, 1462–1874* (Oxford, 1985), and William C. Fuller, *Strategy and Power in Russia, 1600–1914* (New York, 1992).

5. See Arcadius Kahan, *The Plow, the Hammer, and the Knout: An Economic History of Eighteenth-Century Russia* (Chicago, 1985), chap. 3.

6. See Richard Pipes, *Russia under the Old Regime* (New York, 1974; reprinted 1990, 1995), pp. 115–125.

7. Michel Mollat du Jourdin, *Europe and the Seas,* trans. Teresa L. Fagan (Cambridge, Mass., 1993), pp. 153ff., 174. For the North Sea–Baltic world in particular, see David Kirby and Merja-Liisa Hinkkanen, *The Baltic and the North Seas* (London and New York, 2000).

8. David Loades, *The Tudor Navy: An Administrative, Political, and Military History* (Aldershot, England, and Brookfield, Vt., 1992); Bernard Capp, *Cromwell's Navy: The Fleet and the English Revolution* (Oxford, England, and New York, 1989).

9. J. S. Bromley and A. N. Ryan, "Navies," in *The New Cambridge Modern History*, pp. 790–793; Richard Harding, *Seapower and Naval Warfare, 1650–1830* (London and Annapolis, Md., 1999), chaps. 4–6.

10. T. J. Willan, *The Early History of the Russia Company* (Manchester, England, 1956); Jonathan I. Israel, *Dutch Primacy in World Trade, 1585–1740* (Oxford, England, 1989); Anthony Cross, *By the Banks of the Neva: Chapters from the Lives and Careers of the British in Eighteenth-Century Russia* (Cambridge, England, 1997), pp. 44ff.

11. A story told in G. V. Scammell, *The First Imperial Age: European Overseas Expansion, 1400–1715* (Boston, 1989); Carlo M. Cipolla, *Guns, Sails and Empires: Technological Innovation and the Early Phases of European Expansion, 1400–1700* (New York, 1965, 1996); J. H. Parry, *The Age of Reconnaissance* (London, 1963).

12. Peter's draft is printed in N. G. Ustrialov, *Istoriia tsarstvovaniia Petra Velikago,* 1 (St. Petersburg, 1858), pp. 397–401.

13. *PiB,* 1, nos. 14–18 (pp. 15–17) and p. 490. For the full title of this collection of Peter's papers, see Chapter 1, n. 3.

14. John Perry, *The State of Russia under the Present Czar* (London, 1716), p. 164.

15. L. N. Maikov, ed., *Rasskazy Nartova o Petre Velikom* (St. Petersburg, 1891), p. 10.

16. Jan Glete, *Navies and Nations: Warships, Navies and State Building in Europe and America, 1500–1860* (Stockholm, 1993), p. 135; also Harding, *Seapower and Naval Warfare,* pp. 135, 144.

17. Kahan, *The Plow, the Hammer, and the Knout,* pp. 163–266; also Cross, *By the Banks of the Neva.*

18. Cracraft, *Revolution in Architecture,* p. 121.

19. C. A. G. Bridge, ed., *History of the Russian Fleet during the Reign of Peter the Great, by a Contemporary Englishman (1724)* (London, 1899; vol. 15 of Publications of the Navy Records Society), pp. 114, 130–132. The author has since been identified as Captain John Deane.

20. Phillips, *Founding of Russia's Navy,* p. 127.

21. Hughes, *Age of Peter,* p. 81.

22. I. P. Eremin, ed., *Feofan Prokopovich: sochineniia* (Moscow and Leningrad, 1961), p. 106.

23. M. Sarantola-Weiss, "Peter the Great's First Boat: A Symbol of Petrine Influence in Imperial Russia," in Maria DiSalvo and Lindsey Hughes, eds., *A Window on Russia: Papers from the V International Conference of the Study Group on Eighteenth-Century Russia* (Rome, 1996), pp. 37–38, 41.

24. D. Martin, "Ship of State, State of Mind," *New York Times*, Feb. 14, 1997, p. A19.

25. Description with photo in *New York Times*, Jan. 25, 1997, p. A12.

3. Diplomatic and Bureaucratic Revolutions

1. See Charles Tilly, ed., *The Formation of National States in Western Europe* (Princeton, N.J., 1975), a collaborative work by nine leading political scientists and historians; quotations above are from Tilly's summary chapter, "Reflections on the History of European State-Making" (pp. 3–83). For the diplomatic revolution in early modern Europe, see the classic work by Garrett Mattingly, *Renaissance Diplomacy*, first published in Boston in 1955.

2. Tilly, *The Formation of National States*, pp. 42, 73, 74–75. In asserting the crucial linkage between warfare and modern state-building, Tilly draws particularly on the long essay by his collaborator, S. E. Finer, "State- and Nation-Building in Europe: The Role of the Military" (ibid., pp. 84–163), whose generalizations are based primarily on intensive study of early modern France, England, and Brandenburg-Prussia. Finer himself later provided a general account of the rise of the modern state in Europe in his major study, *A History of Government from the Earliest Times*, 3 vols. (Oxford, England, 1997), vol. 2, pt. 2.

3. H. H. Gert and C. Wright Mills, eds. and trans., *From Max Weber: Essays in Sociology* (New York, 1946), pp. 196–204.

4. Nancy S. Kollmann, *Kinship and Politics: The Making of the Muscovite Political System, 1345–1547* (Stanford, 1987), p. 147; Valerie A. Kivelson, *Autocracy in the Provinces: The Muscovite Gentry and Political Culture in the Seventeenth Century* (Stanford, 1996), p. 8.

5. For the royal icons in question see Cracraft, *Revolution in Imagery*, pls. 7, 11, and the related discussion on pp. 114–115, 190–191. For a vigorous presentation of Muscovite patrimonialism see Richard Pipes, *Russia under the Old Regime* (New York, 1974; reprinted 1990, 1995), chaps. 2–4; for the role of the church, see Pipes, *Russia under the Old Regime*, chap. 9.

6. Muscovy's urban network in a comparative international perspective is depicted in Gilbert Rozman, *Urban Networks in Russia, 1750–1800, and Premodern Periodization* (Princeton, N.J., 1976), pp. 56–57; see also Pipes, *Russia under the Old Regime*, pp. 191–211.

7. See Marc Raeff, *The Well-Ordered Police State: Social and Institutional Change through Law in the Germanies and Russia, 1600–1800* (New Haven, Conn., 1983), especially pp. 20–22 for general comments and pp. 43ff. for the German case, with numerous further references.

8. A detailed account of Peter's governmental reforms is in Hughes, *Age of Peter,* chaps. 3, 4. An extremely detailed account of the politics of Peter's reign is in Bushkovitch, *Peter the Great,* all ten chapters plus Epilogue and Conclusion.

9. The most thorough treatment of Peter's abolition of the patriarchate and creation of the Holy Synod is still Cracraft, *Church Reform.*

10. See Cracraft, *Revolution in Imagery,* especially pp. 257ff.

11. Raeff, *The Well-Ordered Police State,* pp. 181–221.

12. Lewitter, *Pososhkov,* pp. 15, 39ff., 50, 73.

13. Pipes, *Russia under the Old Regime,* chap. 5; Anisimov, *Reforms of Peter,* pp. 143–169.

14. See H. M. Scott, in Euan Cameron, ed., *Early Modern Europe* (Oxford, 1999), p. 314; and A. F. Upton, *Charles XI and Swedish Absolutism* (Cambridge, England, 1998), especially chap. 3. See further Paul K. Monod, *The Power of Kings: Monarchy and Religion in Europe, 1589–1715* (New Haven, Conn., 1999); and Leonard Krieger, *Kings and Philosophers, 1689–1789* (New York, 1970), a classic work on the subject.

15. The extent of Prokopovich's authorship remains unresolved: see James Cracraft, "Did Feofan Prokopovich Really Write *Pravda voli monarshei?" Slavic Review* 40, no. 2 (Summer 1981), pp. 173–193.

16. A scholarly English edition has been published by Anthony Lentin, *Peter the Great: His Law on the Imperial Succession in Russia, 1722* (Oxford, 1996).

17. *Pravda,* Lentin edition, pp. 184, 186–187, 188.

18. Ibid., p. 144.

19. See William E. Butler, ed., *A Discourse Concerning the Just Causes of the War between Sweden and Russia: 1700–1721, by P. P. Shafirov* (Dobbs Ferry, N.Y., 1973), reproducing in facsimile both the contemporary English translation and the 1717 Russian original.

20. Ibid. (editor's introduction), p. 7.

21. Ibid. (Russian original), pp. 22, 5.

22. Peter Barber, *Diplomacy: The World of the Honest Spy* (London, 1979), p. 32, no. 35.

4. Cultural Revolution

1. Patrick Collinson, *The Religion of Protestants: The Church in English Society, 1559–1625* (Oxford, England, 1984), p. 1; Emmet Kennedy, *A Cultural History of the French Revolution* (New Haven, Conn., 1989); Sheila Fitzpatrick, ed., *Cultural Revolution in Russia, 1928–1931* (Bloomington, Ind., 1984); Steven Shapin, *The Scientific Revolution* (Chicago, 1996).

2. Most of the material presented in this chapter is taken from Cracraft, *Revolution in Architecture;* Cracraft, *Revolution in Imagery;* and Cracraft, *Revolution in Culture.* Hereafter these volumes will be cited only in instances of direct quotation.

3. Quoted in Cracraft, *Revolution in Architecture,* p. 1.

4. Ibid., pp. 56–61, quoting (p. 60) Christopher Duffy, *Siege Warfare: The Fortress in the Early Modern World, 1494–1660* (London, 1979), p. 173.

5. Cracraft, *Revolution in Architecture,* p. 114, citing an unpublished memoir by Gordon now at the British Library, London.

6. Quoted in ibid., p. 119.

7. Samuel H. Baron, ed. and trans., *The Travels of Olearius in Seventeenth-Century Russia* (Stanford, 1967), p. 113.

8. Cracraft, *Revolution in Architecture,* p. 25, quoting a German visitor of 1684–1686.

9. John Perry, *The State of Russia under the Present Czar* (London, 1716), p. 14.

10. Cracraft, *Revolution in Architecture,* pp. 258 and 266 for the decrees quoted, p. 249 for Catherine.

11. Cracraft, *Revolution in Imagery,* pp. 97–98, figs. 12, 13, and pl. 11.

12. Ibid., pp. 136–137, 269, and fig. 24.

13. See Okenfuss, *Diary of Tolstoi,* passim.

14. Cracraft, *Revolution in Imagery,* pp. 140–147, 194 ff.

15. Quoted in ibid., p. 257.

16. Alison Hilton, *Russian Folk Art* (Bloomington, Ind., 1995).

17. See Elizabeth L. Eisenstein, *The Printing Revolution in Early Modern Europe* (Cambridge, England, 1984)—a digest of her earlier two-volume, now classic work on the subject.

18. Gary Marker, *Publishing, Printing, and the Origins of Intellectual Life in Russia* (Princeton, N.J., 1985), chap. 1.

19. *PiB*, I, no. 291 (pp. 328–331). For the full title of this collection of Peter's papers, see Chapter 1, n. 3.

20. See Cracraft, *Revolution in Culture*, especially chap. 6 and Appendix II: the latter lists about 1,000 words, still current, that were first fixed in Russian in Peter's time together with another 700 or so derivations.

21. Valentin Boss, *Newton and Russia: The Early Influence, 1698–1796* (Cambridge, Mass., 1972), pp. 93–96, reprinting both the original Latin and English versions of the communication.

22. John T. Alexander, "Medical Developments in Petrine Russia," in Cracraft, *Peter Transforms Russia*, p. 194.

23. B. Haigh, "Design for a Medical Service: Peter the Great's Admiralty Regulations (1722)," *Medical History* 19 (1975), pp. 129–146.

24. M. V. Unkovskaya, "Learning Foreign Mysteries: Russian Pupils of the Aptekarskii Prikaz, 1650–1700," *Oxford Slavonic Papers* 30 (1997), pp. 1–20.

25. As reported by Jacob von Stählin (Staehlin), a member of the Academy from 1735 until his death in 1785, in his book *Original Anecdotes of Peter the Great* (London, 1788; first published in German, 1785), p. 344.

26. See Alexander Vucinich, *Science in Russian Culture: A History to 1860* (Stanford, Calif., 1963), pp. 71–76; also J. L. Black, *G.-F. Müller and the Imperial Russian Academy* (Kingston, Ontario, 1986), pp. 7–13. G. F. Müller, the subject of Black's biography, was a history graduate of Leipzig University and one of the first student-teachers to be appointed to the St. Petersburg Academy, where he arrived in November 1725 and remained until his death (in Moscow) in 1783, compiling a distinguished record as a geographer and ethnographer as well as a historian.

27. Vucinich, *Science in Russian Culture*, pp. 181, 182–183; see also Vucinich, *Empire of Knowledge: The Academy of Sciences of the USSR (1917–1970)* (Berkeley and Los Angeles, 1984), with a lengthy introductory chapter on the period 1725–1917. M. D. Gordin, "The Importation of Being Earnest: The Early St. Petersburg Academy of Sciences," *Isis* 91, no. 1 (March 2000), pp. 1–31, also argues for the wider social and cultural significance of the Academy's foundation.

5. Revolution and Resistance

1. Hughes, *Age of Peter,* pp. 454–456. For the earlier history of the *streltsy,* see Richard Hellie, *Enserfment and Military Change in Muscovy* (Chicago, 1971), with numerous references.

2. See Orest Subtelny, *The Mazepists: Ukrainian Separatism in the Early Eighteenth Century* (Boulder, Colo., and New York, 1981), for this story; and further, Zenon E. Kohut, *Russian Centralism and Ukrainian Autonomy: Imperial Absorption of the Hetmanate, 1760s–1830s* (Cambridge, Mass., 1988).

3. Cracraft, *Church Reform,* pp. 19–20 (Avraamy affair); Bushkovitch, *Peter the Great,* pp. 188–197 (Tsykler and others).

4. Details from James Cracraft, "Opposition to Peter the Great," in Ezra Mendelsohn and Marshall S. Shatz, eds., *Imperial Russia, 1700–1917: State, Society, Opposition* (DeKalb, Ill., 1988), pp. 22–36. See also Hughes, *Age of Peter,* pp. 447–461; Cracraft, *Church Reform,* pp. 130, 240–241, 295 (Talitsky affair); and Bushkovitch, *Peter the Great* (most of this long, extremely detailed book is devoted to instances of opposition to Peter from within the ruling elite).

5. The decree is one of a dozen or more from the Petrine period translated in James Cracraft, ed., *Major Problems in the History of Imperial Russia* (Boston, 1994), pp. 110–123 (see p. 110).

6. The struggle is a prominent theme of Anisimov, *Empress Elizabeth.* On noble landowning, see Lee A. Farrow, "Peter the Great's Law of Single Inheritance: State Imperatives and Noble Resistance," *Russian Review* 55, no. 3 (July 1996), pp. 430–447, and Michelle Lamarche Marrese, *A Woman's Kingdom: Noblewomen and the Control of Property in Russia, 1700–1861* (Ithaca, N.Y., 2002).

7. See, for example, Maureen Perrie, *Pretenders and Popular Monarchism in Early Modern Russia* (Cambridge, England, 1995).

8. This is the main theme of Anisimov, *Reforms of Peter.* The centuries-long controversy in Russia over the reign of Peter is thoroughly discussed in Riasanovsky, *Image of Peter.*

9. See Olga Semyonova Tian-Shanskaia, *Village Life in Late Tsarist Russia,* ed. David L. Ransel (Bloomington, Ind., 1993), and Cathy A. Frierson, *Peasant Icons: Representations of Rural People in Late Nineteenth Century Russia* (New York, 1993).

10. Recent works in English, with extensive reference to the Russian scholarship, include Christine D. Worobec, *Peasant Russia: Family and Community in the Post-Emancipation Period* (Princeton, N.J., 1991); and David Moon, *The Russian Peasantry, 1600–1930: The World the Peasants Made* (London and New York, 1999).

11. Robinson, *Rural Russia* (1967 ed., Berkeley and Los Angeles), pp. 126, 258, 244, 2.

12. "Nests of gentility" alludes to Ivan Turgenev's famous novel of this title, *Dvorianskoe gnezdo,* first published 1859.

13. Ibid., pp. 1–2. See further Priscilla Roosevelt's well-illustrated volume *Life on the Russian Country Estate: A Social and Cultural History* (New Haven, Conn., 1995).

14. See Anisimov, *Reforms of Peter,* especially pp. 3–9, 295–298.

6. St. Petersburg

1. Lincoln, *Sunlight at Midnight,* p. 27.

2. Details here and below from Cracraft, *Revolution in Architecture,* pp. 173–174; for details of St. Petersburg's founding, see also Hughes, *Age of Peter,* pp. 210–211.

3. Arcadius Kahan, *The Plow, the Hammer, and the Knout: An Economic History of Eighteenth-Century Russia* (Chicago, 1985), pp. 87, 163, 247–248.

4. Lincoln, *Sunlight at Midnight,* pp. 52, 60.

5. Hughes, *Age of Peter,* pp. 117–119.

6. See further Simon Karlinsky, *Russian Drama from Its Beginnings to the Age of Pushkin* (Berkeley, Calif., 1985); Gerald R. Seaman, *History of Russian Music,* vol. 1 (Oxford, 1967); and Vladimir Morosan, *Choral Performance in Pre-Revolutionary Russia,* revised ed. (Madison, Conn., 1994), for solid introductions to these subjects.

7. Friedrich Christian Weber, *The Present State of Russia,* authorized English translation from the original German, vol. 1 (London, 1723), p. 148.

8. See, for example, Gary Marker and Rachel May, eds. and trans., *Days of a Russian Noblewoman: The Memories of Anna Labzina, 1758–1821* (DeKalb, Ill., 2001).

9. For the *Mirror,* see Cracraft, *Revolution in Culture,* chap. 5; for the quotation from Shafirov's *Discourse,* ibid., chap. 4.

10. From Cracraft, *Revolution in Architecture,* chap. 7.

11. Figures from ibid., pp. 178, 227–228.

12. Ibid., pp. 228, 241, quoting *Lettres du comte Algarotti sur la Russie* (London and Paris, 1769), p. 64.

13. Jonas Hanway, ca. 1745, quoted in Cracraft, *Revolution in Architecture,* p. 232.

14. See Lincoln, *Sunlight at Midnight,* pt. 2.

15. Judith Hemschemeyer, trans., *Selected Poems of Anna Akhmatova,* ed. Roberta Reeder (Brookline, Mass., 2000), p. 101. See further Sharon Leiter, *Akhmatova's Petersburg* (Philadelphia, 1983), and Roberta Reeder, *Anna Akhmatova, Poet and Prophet* (New York, 1994).

Conclusion

1. Earlier conjectures by historians that Peter's measures in support of the army and navy greatly impoverished the masses have been refuted by more recent research. This is not to say that their economic condition improved under Peter, but rather that the evidence is inconclusive on this point.

2. See further Hughes, *Age of Peter,* pp. 186–202.

Further Reading

These suggestions are confined to books in English that provide further details, discussion, and references regarding the reign of Peter the Great. Various other relevant works—specialized monographs, scholarly articles, or books on related subjects—are identified in the notes to the chapters.

Anderson, M. S. *Peter the Great,* 2nd ed. (London and New York: Longman, 1995). A reliable, short yet comprehensive account, biographical in approach, of Peter's reign. First published in 1978.

Anisimov, Evgenii V. *The Reforms of Peter the Great: Progress through Coercion in Russia,* trans. John T. Alexander (Armonk, N.Y.: M. E. Sharpe, 1993). Anisimov is the leading Petrine historian of his generation in Russia; this is a somewhat condensed translation of a book first published in Russian in 1989.

———. *Empress Elizabeth, Her Reign and Her Russia, 1741–1761,* trans. John T. Alexander (Gulf Breeze, Fla.: Academic International Press, 1995). A lively history of the reign of Peter's daughter, emphasizing the role of the nobility.

Black, J. L. *G.-F. Müller and the Imperial Russian Academy* (Kingston and Montreal: McGill-Queen's University Press, 1986). A detailed history of the St. Petersburg Academy of Sciences in its first decades, focusing on the career of one of its first members.

Bushkovitch, Paul. *Peter the Great: The Struggle for Power, 1671–1725* (Cambridge, England, and New York: Cambridge University Press, 2001). A densely detailed account of the politics of the Russian court from just before Peter's birth to the death of Tsarevich Aleksei.

Cracraft, James. *The Church Reform of Peter the Great* (Stanford: Stanford University Press, 1971).

———. *The Petrine Revolution in Russian Architecture* (Chicago: University of Chicago Press, 1988).

———. *The Petrine Revolution in Russian Imagery* (Chicago: University of Chicago Press, 1997).

———. *The Petrine Revolution in Russian Culture* (Cambridge, Mass.: Harvard University Press, forthcoming). This volume, devoted to verbal culture, summarizes and completes the study of the Petrine cultural revolution undertaken in the two preceding volumes.

———, ed. *Peter the Great Transforms Russia* (Boston: Houghton-Mifflin, 1991). A collection of essays by eighteen historians, Russian and non-Russian, on various aspects of Peter's reign.

Cross, Anthony. *Peter the Great through British Eyes* (Cambridge, England, and New York: Cambridge University Press, 2000).

Hughes, Lindsey. *Sophia, Regent of Russia 1657–1704* (New Haven, Conn., and London: Yale University Press, 1998).

———. *Russia in the Age of Peter the Great* (New Haven, Conn., and London: Yale University Press, 1998). The most comprehensive account of Peter's reign in English, with extensive bibliography, notes, and index.

———. *Peter the Great: A Biography* (New Haven, Conn., and London: Yale University Press, 2002). A short biography digested from the preceding volume.

Keep, John L. H. *Soldiers of the Tsar: Army and Society in Russia, 1462–1874* (Oxford, England: Clarendon Press, 1985). A very detailed study of the subject, with two chapters devoted to Peter "the warrior tsar."

Lewitter, L. R., and A. P. Vlasto, eds. and trans. *Ivan Pososhkov: The Book of Poverty and Wealth* (Stanford, Calif.: Stanford University Press, 1987). Translated edition of a book on Russia, its government, society, and economy, written by a contemporary of Peter, with a long and valuable introduction by Lewitter (pp. 1–150).

Lincoln, W. Bruce. *The Romanovs: Autocrats of All the Russias* (New York: Dial Press, 1981). A lively popular history of Russia in the period of the Empire (Peter to 1917).

———. *Sunlight at Midnight: St. Petersburg and the Rise of Modern Russia* (New York: Basic Books, 2000). The best book in English on the subject.

Massie, Robert K. *Peter the Great* (New York: Knopf, 1980). A popular biography—long, lively, and rich in anecdotes.

The New Cambridge Modern History, vol. 6: *The Rise of Great Britain and Russia, 1688–1725,* ed. J. S. Bromley (Cambridge, England: Cambridge University Press, 1970).

Okenfuss, Max J., ed. and trans. *The Travel Diary of Peter Tolstoi: A Muscovite in Early Modern Europe* (DeKalb, Ill.: Northern Illinois University Press, 1987). Tolstoi (Tolstoy) was a close associate of Peter; his diary, published here in English translation with valuable commentary by Okenfuss, is a detailed record of his travels from Russia to Italy and back in 1697–1699.

Phillips, Edward J. *The Founding of Russia's Navy: Peter the Great and the Azov Fleet, 1688–1714* (Westport, Conn.: Greenwood Press, 1995).

Riasanovsky, Nicholas V. *The Image of Peter the Great in Russian History and Thought* (New York and Oxford, England: Oxford University Press, 1985). A masterly survey of Russian views of Peter from his own time to the late Soviet period.

———. *A History of Russia,* 6th ed. (New York and Oxford, England: Oxford University Press, 2000). The best general textbook of Russian history in English.

Index

Absolute monarchy/absolutism, 2, 26, 63, 65–66, 67–69, 72

Academy of Fine Arts, St. Petersburg, 85, 93, 111, 143, 172

Academy of Sciences, St. Petersburg, 62–63, 96, 106–113, 143–144, 171

Admiralty, 49–50, 108, 138, 142, 149, 152, 170

Admiralty College, 49–50

Admiralty Regulation, 108

Adodurov, V. E., 111

Adrian, patriarch, 62, 170

Akhmatova, Anna, 156, 183n15

Aleksei Mikhailovich, tsar, 2–3, 41, 58, 60, 144, 169

Aleksei Petrovich, tsarevich: relations with Peter, 6, 10, 12–14, 63; trial and death of, 12, 14–15, 120–121, 171; and opposition to Peter, 15–16, 114–115, 119

Alexander-Nevsky Monastery, 51, 140, 141

Algarotti, Count Francesco, 153–155, 183n12

Alphabet reform, 99–103

Ambassadorial Office, 5, 8, 71–72, 102

Anna Ivanovna, empress, 71, 153, 171

Apothecary Office, 108

Arabic numerals, introduction of, 101

Archangel, port of, 16, 39, 43, 44, 47

Architecture: Petrine revolution in, 78, 80–87; in contemporary Europe, 78–80; in pre-Petrine Russia, 79, 82–85

Army, modernization of, 29, 30, 32–37

Asia, Russia in, 164

Astrakhan, uprising at, 116–117, 170

Atlas Russica, 96, 172

Avraamy, priest-monk, 118–119

Azov: campaigns against, 6, 33, 80, 170; projected new town of, 81

Baltic fleet, 27, 46, 48, 49, 51

Baroque art and architecture, 78, 82, 89, 130

Bergholtz, F. W. von, 149–152

Bidloo, Dr. Nicolaas, 108

Black Sea fleet, 46

Blumentrost, Dr. Laurentius, 109–110

Boerhaave, Herman, 107, 109

Bolshevik Revolution, 133, 134, 155, 172

Botik (sailboat) of Peter I: his discovery of, 41–42, 50; subsequent shrine of, 51

Brandt, Carsten, 41–43

Bronze Horseman, statue and poem, 136, 155, 164

Bruce, James (Iakov Brius), 5, 6, 27, 89, 106–107
Bulavin, Kondraty, rebellion of , 117, 170

Calendar reform, 124, 170
Cameralism, 61
Cartography, 95–96
Catherine I, empress, 7, 11–12, 27, 63, 141, 171
Catherine II, empress, 52, 63, 81, 87, 111, 136, 172
Charles XII, king of Sweden (1697–1718), 31, 139
Charlotte, princess, wife of Tsarevich Aleksei, 13, 14, 23, 171
Church, Russian Orthodox: Peter's reform of, 9, 16, 25, 26, 62, 112, 126–127, 142; Peter's mockery of, 17–21, 116–117, 127; cult art of, 93–94
Church Slavonic, 67, 98, 99, 101, 104, 130
Civil alphabet and type, 63, 66, 70, 102–103, 170
Coinage, reform of, 94–95
College of Foreign Affairs, 61, 71
College of War, 34, 61
Colleges (administrative), 49, 61–63, 142, 171; building of, 135, 140
Cossacks, 34, 116, 117, 118
Cyrillic alphabet and type, 66, 99–103

Deschisaux, Pierre, 152–153
Diplomacy: Renaissance origins of, 55; Petrine revolution in, 73–74
Discourse Concerning the [Northern] War, 31, 70–73, 105, 147, 178n19
Dynasticism, 31, 54, 65

Ecclesiastical Regulation, 26, 112, 120, 126, 171
Educational initiatives, 33–34, 48–49, 85, 93, 108, 111–112, 126, 143, 145. See also Naval Academy; School of Mathematics and Navigation, Moscow
Elizabeth I, empress, 10, 11, 27, 52, 93, 155, 172
Emancipation of serfs, 36, 131, 132, 163, 172
Emperor, new Russian title of, 27, 171

Erskine, Dr. Robert, 108–109
Etiquette reform, 145–147
Evdokia Lopukhina, tsaritsa (1669–1731), 10, 120, 170

Farquharson, Henry, 101
Fedor III, tsar, 3, 5, 58, 169
Feofan Prokopovich. See Prokopovich, Feofan
Fiscals (fiskaly), 62, 63
Folk art, 94, 130

General Regulation, 61, 171
German Settlement, Moscow, 4, 6, 8, 10, 17, 21
Gordon, General Patrick, 5–6, 43, 44, 80, 116
Grand Embassy, 6, 39, 45, 70, 85, 90–91, 119, 170
Grotius, Hugo, 67, 68

Hangö Head, Russian naval victory at, 48, 171
Heraldry, 63, 94
Holy Synod, 25, 62, 120–122, 142, 171

Iaguzhinsky, Pavel, 8
Imagery: Petrine revolution in, 63, 87, 89, 93–96; in pre-Petrine Russia, 87, 89–90; in post-Renaissance Europe, 87–89
Imperial Court Choir, 145
Imperial Court Orchestra, 145
Ivan IV the Terrible, tsar (1547–1584), 24, 115, 137
Ivan V, tsar, 3–4, 5, 115, 169, 170

Joachim, patriarch, 3
Judicial reform, failure of, 64

Kliuchevsky, V. O., historian, 20, 174n15
Kneller, Sir Godfrey, 91
Kunstkamera, 107, 109, 135, 141
Kurakin, Prince Boris, 5, 17–18, 20

Law of diplomatic immunity, origins of, 73–74
LeBlond, J.-B. A., 140, 152

Lefort, François ("Frants"), 5–6, 43
Leibniz, Gottfried W., 76, 107
Lomonosov, M. V., 111, 112, 144

Makarov, Aleksei, 8, 9, 27
Matveev, Count Andrei, 73, 89, 93
Mazepa, Hetman Ivan, 118, 170
Medical Chancery, 109
Menshikov, Prince Alexander, 6–8, 91, 145,
    149, 153, 171
Michael Romanov, tsar, 3, 169
Military revolution in early modern
    Europe, 29–31, 79–80
Military Statute, 34, 61, 108, 162, 171
Mons, Anna, 10
Mons, William, 12
Moscow: kremlin (citadel) of, 4, 27, 50, 51,
    59, 79; architecture of, 83, 84; university
    of, 111, 112
Moscow Baroque architecture, 82, 85
Moscow *Gazette,* 102, 138, 170
Muscovy: tsardom of, 1–2, 58–60, 74, 95;
    cultural persistence of, 129–130
Muscovy (later Russia) Company, 39, 40,
    47
Musketeers *(streltsy),* 6, 32, 115–117,
    122–123, 170

Narva: Russian siege of, 32, 137, 170; cap-
    ture of, 138
Natalia Alekseevna, tsarevna, 6, 10–11, 13,
    145, 171
Natalia Naryshkina, tsaritsa, 3, 10, 11, 43,
    170
Naval Academy, 46, 48–49, 143, 171
Naval Statute, 41, 43, 44, 50, 61, 162, 171
Navy, creation and deployment of, 29, 37,
    44–48, 50, 52, 53
Nevsky Prospekt, 140, 149
Newton, Isaac, 76, 107
Nobility: in Muscovy, 1, 60, 125; under
    Peter and later, 35–36, 94, 125–126,
    133–134, 162; emancipation of, 36, 163,
    172
Northern War, 31–32, 48, 136–137, 139, 159
Nöteborg, Russian siege of, 48
Nystad (Nystadt), Peace of, 37, 51, 139, 171

Old Believers, 116, 117, 119, 123, 130, 169
Order of St. Andrew, 5, 71
Ottoman empire, 32, 33, 34, 45, 71

Paper mills in Russia, 98
Paris Academy of Sciences, 77–78, 79, 107
Paul I, emperor, 64, 162, 172
Pavlenko, N. I., historian, 7, 173n4
Peasant Russia, 86–87, 130–133
Perry, Captain John, 46, 84
Persian campaign, 35, 47, 171
Peter I, tsar and first emperor: childhood
    and youth, 2–4; opposition to, 4, 6,
    14–16, 115–29, 163; war games of, 6, 17,
    29, 33, 79, 80, 116; and women, 10–12,
    162–163; relations with son Aleksei,
    12–16; amusements of, 16–21, 118–119,
    127; controversial legacy of, 20–21, 24,
    36–37, 64–65, 129; abundant relics of,
    21, 24, 92, 157; speaks Dutch, 21, 38, 72;
    dreams of, 21–24, 161; modern mentality
    of, 22, 41, 69, 161; historical significance
    of, 24, 28, 45, 64–65, 72–73, 160, 164; his
    pietism, 25–26; death and funeral of,
    26–28; his "toy fleet" and growing nauti-
    cal obsession, 41–46, 81; cult of, 53; his
    domik (little house), 82, 135; loves Dutch
    art, 89, 151; takes lessons in etching,
    91–92; father of Russian medicine,
    107–109
Peter II, emperor, 153, 171
Peter III, emperor, 10, 51, 172
Peterhof *(Petrodvorets),* 89, 135, 140, 141,
    151–152
Peter-Paul fortress and church: as signifi-
    cant Petrine site, 15, 23, 27, 52, 135; con-
    struction of, 81–82, 138, 149–150
Peter the Great. *See* Peter I
Petrine elite, 28, 85, 94, 103–104, 106,
    160–161
Petrine revolution, cultural essence of,
    75–77, 103–106, 128–129, 158, 160–161,
    164
Police state, early modern European theory
    of, 64–65
Poltava, battle of, 8, 71, 118, 170
Postnikov, Peter, 108

Pravda voli monarshei (Right of the Monarch's Will), 66–70
Preobrazhenskoe, royal estate of, 4, 20, 42, 80; guards regiment founded at, 6, 8, 115; as headquarters of political police, 115, 119–122, 170
Print revolution: in early modern Europe, 90; in Russia, 97–103
Prokopovich, Feofan, 9–10, 26, 27–28, 44, 50–51, 66, 171
Pruth river, battle by, 34–35, 46, 71, 81, 139, 171
Pugachev rebellion, 117, 172
Pushkin, Alexander, 136, 155, 156, 164

Razin rebellion, 117, 169
Renaissance art and architecture, 78, 87–89
Robinson, G. T., historian, 131–134, 182nn11–13
Romanov dynasty, 3, 31, 63–64
Romodanovsky, Prince Fedor, 5, 17, 19, 43
Royal (English) Navy, 38–39
Royal Society, London, 40, 106–107
Russian, modern (language), dates to Peter, 103–106, 111–113, 130
Ruysch, Dr. Fredrik, 107

St. Petersburg: founding and early construction of, 22, 35, 81–83, 136–141, 150, 170; as military and naval base, 33–34, 41, 46, 49; as major port, 36, 47, 142; as "window on Europe," 48, 155; renamed Leningrad, 52, 137, 156; as new capital, 66, 74, 142–143, 153, 155; as cultural center, 81–83, 86, 93, 143–147; population of, 82, 83, 143, 150, 155; historical significance of, 83, 86, 136, 141–147, 164–165; university of, 112, 135; as monument to Peter, 135–136, 156; contemporary descriptions of, 147–155; renamed Petrograd, 155
School of Mathematics and Navigation, Moscow, 40, 46, 101, 170
Schoonebeck, Adriaan, 92
Secret Chancellery (Chancellery for Secret Inquisitorial Affairs), 14–15, 120, 121, 128

Senate, 61–62, 142, 171
Serfdom, 36, 59, 60, 123, 131
Shafirov, Baron Peter, 8–9, 12, 31, 70–72, 147
Shumacher, J. D., 109–110
Sophia, grand princess (1657–1704), 4, 6, 33, 115, 119, 123, 170
Sovereign state, European origins of, 54–57
Succession law, 63–64, 67, 171
Sumarokov, Alexander, 144

Table of Ranks, 35, 61, 162, 171
Talitsky, Grigory, 121–122
Tapestry, 94
Taxation, 34, 63, 171
Teplov, G. N., 111
Tessing, Jan, 100
Tilly, Charles, historian, 155, 177nn1, 2
Time of Troubles, 2, 3, 98, 169
Timmerman, Franz, 41–43
Tolstoy (Tolstoi), Count Peter, 5, 14, 15, 92
Trediakovsky, V. K., 11, 112, 144
Trezzini, Dominico, 82, 135, 139–140

Ukrainian separatism, 118
Ulozhenie (law code), 60, 64, 98, 169

Verbal culture, Petrine revolution in, 96–106, 130
Vignola, *Rule of the Five Orders of Architecture*, 78, 86, 141
Voronezh, 44–45, 49, 81, 83

Ward, Mrs. Thomas, 153
Weber, F. C., 18, 145–146, 148, 174n2, 182n7
Weber, Max, on bureaucracy, 57
Whitworth, Charles, 147–148
William III, prince of Orange and king of England (1689–1702), 38
Winter Palace, 27, 135, 141

Yavorsky, Stefan, 121

Zemtsov, Mikhail, 140
Zotov, Nikita, 17, 18
Zubov, Aleksei, 92